PINELANDS FOLKLIFE

A project of the New Jersey State Council on the Arts,
the New Jersey Historical Commission,
and the New Jersey State Museum in the Department of State

Co-sponsored by the American Folklife Center at the Library of Congress

Partly funded by a National Endowment for the Humanities planning grant for the exhibition
"New Jersey Pinelands: Tradition and Environment."

PINELANDS

EDITED BY

RITA ZORN MOONSAMMY
DAVID STEVEN COHEN
LORRAINE E. WILLIAMS

FOLKLIFE

RUTGERS UNIVERSITY PRESS
New Brunswick and London

Library of Congress Cataloging-in-Publication Data

Pinelands folklife.

    Includes index.
    1. Pine Barrens (N.J.)—Social life and customs.
2. Pine Barrens (N.J.)—Industries.   3. Handicraft—
New Jersey—Pine Barrens.   I. Moonsammy, Rita Zorn.
II. Cohen, David Steven, 1943–   .   III. Williams, Lorraine E.
F142.P5P56   1987   974.9   86–6713
ISBN 0–8135–1188–7
ISBN 0–8135–1189–5 (pbk.)

British Cataloging-in-Publication Information Available.

CONTENTS

INTRODUCTION

RITA MOONSAMMY, DAVID S. COHEN, LORRAINE E. WILLIAMS

I

TELLING THE LANDSCAPE:

Folklife Expressions and Sense of Place

MARY T. HUFFORD

13

CREATING THE LANDSCAPE:

Historic Human Ecology of the Pinelands

JOHN W. SINTON

43

LIVING WITH THE LANDSCAPE:

Folklife in the Environmental Subregions of the Pinelands

RITA MOONSAMMY, DAVID S. COHEN, MARY T. HUFFORD

65

ILLUSTRATIONS

MAPS

FOREWORD

This book stands at a confluence that, like Barnegat Bay, has many feeder streams of private and public initiative. The well-spring of these many initiatives in turn has been the abiding interest of local people in maintaining their way of life, and the equally abiding curiosity of others from the outside world to learn more about it.

My own relationship with the region began in 1977, when the Pinelands National Reserve was first considered by the Congress and the American Folklife Center was less than two years old. At the urging of Douglass College folklorist Angus Gillespie, my wife and I visited Waretown and the surrounding area. "You've got to come to Albert Hall," Angus said, knowing I play the fiddle and love folk music. So we attended the Saturday-night program at Albert Hall, where members of the Pinelands Cultural Society played an amiable concert of homespun music to an appreciative audience of locals and visitors. Like thousands of visitors to the Pinelands before and after us, we received our first glimpse of its culture through the Pinelands Cultural Society.

In 1977 the national impulse to save the New Jersey Pine Barrens was grounded in ecological and recreational concerns. Then, as now, many people actually thought that there was no real culture in the Pine Barrens—nothing beyond a few remnants of the region's nineteenth-century industrial heyday. The members of the Pinelands Cultural Society wanted to save the Pine Barrens, too, but their concern was for their cultural traditions. They sensed that, unless some official vehicle could be found for recognizing local culture, the cultural treasures of South Jersey would be overshadowed by Pine Barrens tree frogs and curly grass ferns in the public image of, and the planning for, the region. The Society knew that in order to protect their culture they had to start articulating it to outsiders and to each other. When they hosted my visit to Albert Hall, they were asking the government to acknowledge the worth of their traditional life and values by documenting South Jersey culture with the same care that it devoted to resources of scientific value.

Albert Hall had its roots in weekly musical gatherings that developed in the 1960s at Joe and George Albert's hunting cabin in the Forked River Mountains. At George Albert's funeral his musical friends decided to establish a permanent, formal gathering place and to name it in honor of the Albert brothers. Remembering the famed music hall in London, they chose the name Albert Hall. Thus a place was established for the formal presentation of the Pinelands' heritage and values.

At the Saturday Night Jamborees in the old warehouse on Route 9 in Waretown that constitutes the temporary Albert Hall, themes similar to those that animate this book are evident. The ancestors of the people onstage sailed as sea captains, operated water-powered sawmills, mined and logged cedar, and converted hundreds of acres of pine into charcoal. They themselves have built sneakboxes and garveys, fought forest fires, trapped snapping turtles, clammed in the bays, lumbered in the swamps, chased foxes on the plains, and harvested muskrats and salt hay in the meadows. They are the custodians of their culture and of their landscapes, of which the Pineconers sing:

> Beyond the mountain to the meadow, from the river to
>   the bay—
> Beloved by folks of yesteryear and those right here today;
> The Pines along the Jersey shore seem to be the greenest
>   here—
> The lakes with sparkling beauty bring us joy throughout
>   the year.

This excerpt from the song "A Piney's Lament," by Janice Sherwood, is part of a large repertoire of original compositions that teach visitors to Albert Hall about local life and traditional values, that preserve and celebrate important places, events, and sentiments in the collective memory: "The Pine Barrens Song," "The Clamdigger," "A Home in the Pines," "Proud to be a Piney," "The Ballad of Julie Jane," "Forked River Mountain Blues," "Pines of Bamber," "My Double Trouble Queen," "Have You Ever Been Out on the Bay," "Jersey Moon," "Beautiful Barnegat Bay," and "Come on Down to Waretown."

Over the past decade public concern for "local lifeways" in the Pinelands has been catching up with the international interest in the region's special flora, fauna, and geology. In 1977 Linda Buki at the New Jersey State Council on the Arts inaugurated a Folk-Artists-in-Schools program in Burlington County. Building on research by folklorists Patricia Averill and Angus Gillespie, the program placed suburban students in contact with Pine Barrens traditions such as cranberry harvesting, boat building, clamming, the music of the Pineconers, and the stories of David Ridgway. From 1979 to 1983 the understanding of the region gathered force through school programs in Ocean and Cumberland counties conducted by Mary Hufford and Rita Moonsammy. These programs featured many of the traditions and tradition-bearers highlighted in this book: boatbuilding, salt haying, trapping, lumbering, clamming, oystering, fishing, cranberrying, mossing, gathering, charcoal making, fox hunting, decoy carving, quilting, cooking, singing, storytelling, and glassblowing.

Clearly, the region was rich with traditional life and well stocked with indigenous teachers; clearly, the living cultural traditions deserved a systematic survey. The foundations were already in place: the surveys and mapping of natural resources by scientists for the Pinelands Commission, the development of a human ecological model of the region by Jonathan Berger and John Sinton, and a regional network of tradition-bearers uncovered by state folk arts and folklife projects. In 1983 the American Folklife Center brought several years of discussion with the Pinelands Commission and the National Park Service to fruition by launching the Pinelands Folklife Project. The project's first task was to create an archive, a collection of documentary materials that would survey and preserve evidence of the traditional life of the region. An archive could not only document the cultural life of the region today, but could also provide a kind of map for the commission—making cultural signposts visible; illuminating the junctures of landscape, history, and traditional life and thought; and providing a cultural perspective for the decision making about the region's future.

Now we have a book to carry us a step farther. Its publication is timed to coincide with the January 1987 opening of the exhibition "New Jersey Pinelands: Tradition and Environment"; together they will synthesize and make public the great volume of work that has been generated over the past decade. The State Museum, the Historical Commission, and the Arts Council have rendered an important service by creating such fine vehicles for sharing the collaborative research of so many agencies and individuals. The book and the exhibition are partly for people who still think that there is no culture in South Jersey. But mostly they are for the people of the Pinelands, who want to keep their cultural traditions alive and who have the most at stake in our better understanding of those traditions. We are pleased to have had a part in presenting the landscape that is the magnum opus of their life and thought.

Alan Jabbour, Director
American Folklife Center
The Library of Congress

ACKNOWLEDGMENTS

Many people and organizations were involved in the publication of this book and in the preparation of the exhibition that accompanies it. We wish to express our thanks to them and acknowledge their contributions.

The staff of the American Folklife Center at the Library of Congress has been helpful in many ways throughout this project. Pinelands Folklife Project Director Mary Hufford provided assistance in formulating ideas, retrieving materials, and identifying resources.

The fieldworkers who participated in the Pinelands Folklife Project, and who also consulted with us during the preparation of the manuscript, included Thomas Carroll, the late Christine Cartwright, Carl Fleischhauer, Eugene Hunn, Jens Lund, Bonnie Blair O'Connor, Mal O'Connor, Gerald E. Parsons, Nora Rubinstein, Susan Samuelson, and Elaine Thatcher.

Photographs were taken by Joseph Czarnecki, Carl Fleischhauer, and Dennis McDonald for the American Folklife Center, by Joseph Crilley and Anthony Masso for the New Jersey State Museum, and by Michael Bergman for the New Jersey State Council on the Arts.

The staff of the Pinelands Commission assisted in locating resources for both the exhibition and the book.

Others who consulted with us about the project are William Bolger, Betsy Carpenter, Herbert Halpert, Donald Pettifer, George H. Pierson, Edward S. Rutsch, John Sinton, Gaye Taylor, Paul J. Taylor, Eugene Vivian, and Elizabeth M. Woodford.

Beryl Robichaud deserves special thanks for supplying much of the natural history material.

Librarians and archivists who retrieved information and photographs for us included Ronald Becker, Charles Cummings, Rebecca Colesar, Barbara S. Irwin, Carol Lapinsky, Robert Looney, Carl Niederer, Kathy Stavick, and Edward Skipworth.

The local historians Patricia H. Burke, John Callery, Somers Corson, Herbert Vanaman, Barbara Koedel, Everett Mickle, Polly Miller, Mary Ann Thompson, Sarah Watson, Carl West, and Joseph Wilson also helped in the project.

Staff at the New Jersey State Museum who worked on the project were Zoltan Buki, Suzanne Crilley, Wallace Conway, Karen Flinn, David Parris, and Cater Webb.

Curators at other museums and collections included Martin Decker, Alan Frazier, Thomas F. Harrington, John Hines, Ruth Hyde, Craig Mabius, and Rick Mitchell.

The following administrators of the cosponsoring agencies provided guidance and encouragement: Jeffrey A. Kesper and Barbara Russo at the New Jersey State Council on the Arts; Bernard Bush, Richard Waldron, and Howard Green at the New Jersey Historical Commission; Leah P. Sloshberg at the New Jersey State Museum; and Alan Jabbour at the American Folklife Center.

Support staff who helped with the manuscript were Elizabeth A. Crummey, Darin Oliver, Linda L. Tate, and Dolores Truchon at the New Jersey State Council on the Arts, Evelyn Taylor and Patricia Thomas at the New Jersey Historical Commission, and Gina Giambrone at the New Jersey State Museum.

Individuals who lent objects and photographs from their private collections to the exhibition include Frank Astemborski, Margaret Bakely, Tom Brown, Owen Carney, Les Christofferson, Hurley Conklin, John DuBois, Clifford Frazee, Steve Frazee, Walter Earling, Father Konstantin Federov, Lillian Rae Gerber, Albertson Huber, Jean Jones, Leo Landy, Dorothy Lilly, Ted Ramp, Michelle Rappoport, Joe Reid, Anne Salmons, Mary Ann Thompson, Virginia Durell Way, and Helen Zimmer. Many of these people deserve additional thanks for providing us with important background information, as well.

Organizations that lent objects and photographs include the Atlantic County Historical Society, Agricultural Museum of the State of New Jersey, Batsto Citizens Committee, Batsto Village State Historic Site, Burlington County Historical Society, Cape May Historical Society, Cumberland County Historical Society, Deserted Village at Allaire, Donald A. Sinclair Special Collections of the Alexander Library at Rutgers University, Gloucester County Historical Society, Hammonton Historical Society, Medford Historical Society, Monmouth County Historical Association, Newark Public Library, New Jersey Bureau of Forest Management in the Division of Parks and Forestry, New Jersey Division of Archives and Records Management, New Jersey Historical Society, New Jersey Pinelands Commission, New Jersey State Library, Ocean County Historical Society, Office of New Jersey Heritage in the Division of Parks and Forestry, and Wheaton Historical Association.

Many other people shared their knowledge of the Pinelands during interviews and the planning phase of this exhibition and book. They include Joe Albert, Fenton Anderson, Belford Blackman, George Brewer, Jr., Patricia Burke, Ken Camp, George Campbell, Larry Carpenter, Jack Cervetto, Milton Collins, Mark Darlington, Anne and Jack Davis, Frank Day, Charles De Stefano, Miguel Juan de Jesus, John Earlin, Eugene Espinosa, Lehma and Ed Gibson, Richard Gille, Lydia Gonzalez, Ed Hazelton, George Heinrichs, John A. Hillman, Nerallen Hoffman, Sam Hunt, Norman Jeffries, Malcolm Jones, Mary and Ed Lamonaca, Hazel and Leo Landy, Abbott, Stephen III, and Stephen Lee, Jr., Leonard Maglioccio, George Marquez, Haines, Henry, and Francis Mick, Herb Misner, Burtis Myers, Jr., Clara Paolino, Gladys and Harry Payne, Herbert Payne, Lou Peterson, Valia Petrenko, Charles Pomlear, Bluma Purmell, Ralph Putiri, Albert Reeves, Todd Reeves, David Ridgway, Merce Ridgway, Harry V. Shourds, Jim Stasz, Caroline and Norman Taylor, Brad Thompson, Alice Tomlinson, Orlando Torres, Dusia Tserbotarew, Ted Von Bosse, Lynwood Veach, Bill Wasiowich, Joanne Van Istendal, and Beryl Whittington.

The preparation of the manuscript of this book was partially funded by a planning grant from the National Endowment for the Humanities.

PINELANDS FOLKLIFE

INTRODUCTION

Opposite: *Orlando Torres of Vincentown. Photograph by Carl Fleischhauer. American Folklife Center,* PFP201851-2-29.

MUCH OF THE PINELANDS REGION OF SOUTHERN NEW JERSEY seems to consist only of monotonous stretches of sand and scraggly pine, the basis for both the historic name "Pine Barrens" and the old perception of the area as infertile. Yet the region is neither uniform nor barren. It is rich in both ecological subsystems, such as cedar swamps, meadows (salt- and freshwater marshes), and forests, and natural resources, such as sphagnum moss, fur-bearing animals, and wood. And, partly because of this natural wealth, it is equally rich in folklife. In every subsystem of the Pinelands, residents have built traditional systems of resource cultivation and use that have shaped the landscape and the history of the region.

These traditional technologies, however, are merely one aspect of the folklife of the Pinelands. Like such technologies elsewhere, they are grounded in the "sense of place" of the people of the region. Sense of place is the totality of perceptions and knowledge of a place gained by residents through their long experience in it, and intensified by their feelings for it. It enables them to create indigenous systems for classifying resources, methods for cultivating them, and tools for harvesting them. But sense of place also informs their play and art. Jokes about Jersey mosquitoes, poems about the woods, and paintings of blueberry fields express sense of place and give us a native's eye for the region.

These cultural phenomena, and the people who have created them, are

Rita Moonsammy / David S. Cohen / Lorraine E. Williams

I

Sandy Road in the Pinelands. Photograph by Dennis McDonald. New Jersey State Council on the Arts.

an essential and fascinating, but little told, aspect of the story of the Pinelands. Ideally, the Pinelands people should provide the voice of the story, spoken in the context of the scholar's description of the natural environment and the broad historical patterns of human use of it. That conviction shapes this book, from its overview of the ecological makeup of the region and the changes in perceptions of it, through its essays on sense of place, human ecology, and traditional activities.

Ecologically, the Pinelands is remarkable for its location, its water system, and its flora and fauna. It stretches over much of the Outer Coastal Plain, that portion of New Jersey that punctuates America's Atlantic coastline like a giant comma, and encompasses one million acres, nearly 20 percent of the state's land area. The Pinelands' northern limits touch Monmouth County, and its southern edges reach down into Cape May County on Delaware Bay, so that a traveler on the Garden State Parkway may survey the varied scenery of the Pinelands National Reserve while riding south from Exit 90 at Bricktown to Exit 12 near Swainton. Not far north, west, and south of the Pinelands are several of the nation's largest cities.

Though travelers on other roads often believe that the region has a tedious sameness, it is actually a large ecosystem embracing a variety of very different, yet closely interrelated subsystems: forests, hardwood swamps, spungs (cedar bogs), streams, ponds, salt- and freshwater meadows, rivers, and bays.[1] Its most crucial and remarkable feature is the Cohansey Aquifer, a body of groundwater with a storage capacity believed to be as much as 17 trillion gallons. The aquifer links the various subsystems, from the dry, sandy uplands, where the water table is more than two feet beneath the surface, to soggy wetlands, where it rises to or above the soil surface.

The geological formation that holds the water is called the Cohansey Sand; generally, its soils are coarse, loose, and low in nutrients. Precipitation flows easily through the sandy soil and replenishes the water table, and groundwater seeps just as easily upward to feed the streams. The streams, in turn, coalesce into rivers, which form estuaries where they meet the sea.

But the very ease of water flow within the system also makes it vulnerable to pollution damage. Because this largely unpolluted aquifer is bordered by areas of rapid population growth, its protection is of serious concern to conservationists and natives.

Unusual plants and animals with interesting histories are another important feature of the Pinelands that has also prompted protection efforts. Pyxie moss and the northern pine snake are among more than 100 plants and animals that extended their ranges north thousands of years ago when the sea level was lower and nature provided a broad highway along the coast. Today, the Pines is their northernmost home. Other species—broom crowberry, for instance—extended their ranges southward as tundralike conditions were created by advancing ice sheets.

Still other species are remarkable for having adapted over the centuries to forest fires, which occur regularly in the Pinelands. The pitch pine (*Pinus rigida*), for instance, which dominates the landscape, outcompetes other tree species here because of its thick bark and its ability to put out new shoots from the base of the tree even when the top has been killed by fire.

The histories of some plants are more closely linked to humans, whose landscape artifacts—cranberry bogs, iron forges, mining pits, agricultural fields, and railroad rights-of-way—have left their mark on the Pinelands flora by providing habitats for alien species.

Though the Pinelands is often depicted as uninhabited wilderness, this area has actually been used by humans for many centuries. A thousand years ago, the region was used by the Lenape Indians (also known as the Delaware). These people are assumed to have lived in independent groups of about 100 members, and spoke dialects of the Algonkian language family similar to those of the Native Americans in what are now southern Connecticut, metropolitan New York, eastern Pennsylvania, and northern Delaware.[2] Much of what is now considered traditional culture of the Pinelands—hunting, trapping, fishing and collecting of wild plants—was already Indian tradition when the first Europeans arrived. The Lenape moved seasonally within southern New Jersey to take advantage of the availability of different foods. They fished shad from the rivers in spring, and farmed sandy riverside soils in summer. In fall, they collected nuts from the woodlands, and in fall and winter they hunted white-tailed deer in communal hunts.

Before the arrival of the Europeans, the Lenape probably used the Pinelands mainly as hunting territory. When the Brotherton Reservation was created for them in the eighteenth century at what is now Indian Mills in Burlington County, officials expected them to harvest game and wood from the forests. The reservation was too small a territory to support their seasonal hunting and gathering system, however, and by 1802 most of them either moved west or settled in New York.

By the mid-eighteenth century, the Pinelands supported a number of resource-based industries, and for 150 years the size of the basically Anglo-American population rose and fell with these various industries: lumbering, iron mining and forging, and glassmaking. In the late nineteenth century, however, railroads opened the interior and the coast to development as an agricultural and resort area, and brought European immigrants who established small towns and ethnic agricultural communities. In the twentieth century, the development of the automobile and the desire for homes outside of the cities have brought new residents to the Pinelands, many of whom work elsewhere. Today, therefore, the region has a wide variety of residents and users, including both families who continue to ply traditional occupations and visitors who explore woods and waters.

Over the years, much has been written and said about the people and the place, for the Pinelands has been perceived as unusual since the first travelers passed through. Evaluations of the region have changed, as have ways of defining its boundaries.

During the Colonial period, the region was considered a "barrens," unfit for agriculture. In 1765, in his *History of the Colony of Nova-Caesaria, or New Jersey,* Samuel Smith wrote:

Almost the whole extent of the province adjoining on the atlantick, is barrens, or nearly approaching it; yet there are scattered settlements all along the coast, the people subsisting in great part by cattle in the bog, undrained meadows and marshes, and selling them to graziers, and cutting down the cedars; there were originally plenty of both the white and red sorts: The towring retreat of the former have afforded many an asylum for David's men of necessity. . . . The barrens or poor land, generally continues from the sea up into the province, thirty miles or more, and this nearly the whole extent from east to west; so that there are many thousands areas, that will never serve much the purposes of agriculture; consequently when the pines and cedars are generally gone (they are so already in many places) this will not be of much value.[3]

Although by the late nineteenth century the potential of the region for certain types of agriculture was realized and some evaluations had changed, the people of the Pinelands continued to be regarded in a stereotyped way that can be traced back to the British Isles and Europe, where the forest was considered as a refuge, and the forest dweller as one who did not fit into society.[4] The same notion was applied to both the frontiersman in eighteenth-century America and the "Piney" in nineteenth-century New Jersey. It has persisted into the twentieth century.

Legends about the origins of the people of the Pinelands were created and circulated primarily by people who lived outside the area. They variously claimed that Pineys were descended from disaffected Quakers who had rejected the tenets of the Society of Friends; Tories who had sided with the British during the Revolutionary War; mercenary Hessian soldiers who deserted the British army during the same era; pirates, smugglers, privateers, and "Pine Robbers" who took advantage of the social unrest during the Revolution to plunder and steal; and Indians from the Brotherton Reservation.

In fact, the people of the Pinelands are descended from the same families that settled other areas of South Jersey. They included Dutch, Germans, and English Quakers. The Germans, however, came by way of Pennsylvania well before the Revolutionary War, and had different surnames from those of the Hessians who fought for the British. There is some truth to the claim that smugglers and privateers worked the region, for in the years before the Revolution, smugglers operated along the coast to avoid the British Navigation Acts, and privateers operated out of these same ports during the war. However, there is no evidence that the pirates William Kidd or William Teach ("Blackbeard") ever came to New Jersey, contrary to local legends about buried treasure. Finally, the claim that the Lenape Indians left descendants (with the possible exception of Indian Ann Roberts, a basketmaker from Shamong Township) remains to be proven.[5]

Map of the boundaries of the Pine Barrens and the Pinelands National Reserve.

The stereotype of the Piney was reinforced by the notorious Kallikak study conducted in the first decades of the twentieth century by the Vineland Training School. The study purported to trace two branches of a family that descended from Martin Kallikak (a pseudonym), a Revolutionary War soldier. The "Piney" branch supposedly descended from his alliance with a barmaid and included depraved and feebleminded members. The other branch, however, supposedly intermarried with some of the "best" families in New Jersey.[6] In fact, recent research has proved that the so-called Kallikak family was from Hunterdon County, not from the Pinelands.[7] Yet people thought the study was about the "Pineys," perhaps because Elizabeth Kite, the fieldworker on the Kallikak study, also wrote a report on the people of the Pinelands.

The boundaries of the Pinelands have been defined differently at different times, and the names "Pine Barrens" and "Pinelands" illustrate those differences. In 1916, when botanist John Harshberger published *The Vegetation of the New Jersey Pine Barrens,* he identified the boundaries of the region by vegetation distribution and defined it as bounded on the east and south by bays and salt marsh, and on the north and west by farmlands and hardwood forests. Similar methods were used by other botanists.

Aspects of the region's environment have affected the study of its culture. When folklorist Herbert Halpert, then a graduate student at Indiana University, began his fieldwork in the Pinelands in the 1930s, he adopted Harshberger's concept of its boundaries, but focused on the forests north of the Mullica River rather than the agricultural area south of it. Reasoning that the culture of the farmers would be different from that of people living in the forested areas, Halpert therefore collected data mainly in Burlington and Ocean counties.

Halpert believed that the negative reputation of the people of the Pines reflected a bias of urban people toward rural people, and he set out to record their stories and songs in order to show them through their own expressions. His work took the form of an unpublished dissertation entitled "Folktales and Legends from the New Jersey Pines," and of a folk-song collection which is housed in the Indiana University Archives of Traditional Music.[8] Unfortunately, his collection never reached the general public.

In the 1960s, however, environmentalists began to focus attention on the Pinelands as a unique and sensitive region, and to emphasize the importance of the aquifer. Their view was typified in a popular book entitled *The Pine Barrens.* Its author, John McPhee, portrayed the area as a wilderness "so close to New York that on a very clear night a bright light in the Pines

THE BOUNDARIES OF THE PINE BARRENS AND THE PINELANDS NATIONAL RESERVE

Folklorist Elaine Thatcher interviewing Clara Paolino of Ancora. Photograph by Susan Samuelson. PFP–BSS286558–14–4a. Pinelands Folklife Project Archive, American Folklife Center, Library of Congress. Hereafter, photographs from the archives will be listed with data retrieval number only.

would be visible from the Empire State Building," [9] and stressed the importance of the Cohansey Aquifer as a supply of pure water:

> The water of the Pine Barrens is soft and pure, and there is so much of it that, like the forest above it, it is an incongruity in place and time. In the sand under the pines is a natural reservoir of pure water that, in volume, is the equivalent of a lake seventy-five feet deep with a surface of a thousand square miles. . . . The Pine Barrens rank as one of the greatest natural recharging areas of the world. [10]

Evaluations such as this gave impetus to efforts to preserve the region from rampant development. In the 1960s and 1970s, local, state, and federal agencies began to enact legislation to govern land use and to preserve the natural resources of the region. In 1978, the federal government designated the Pine Barrens as the country's first "national reserve," a protected area in which much of the land remains in private ownership although its use is subject to governmental review. In 1979, the New Jersey Legislature passed the Pinelands Protection Act and created the Pinelands Commission to regulate land use.

The legislative actions resulted in a new map of the area. In consideration of management needs, the National Parks and Recreation Act of 1978 included within the boundaries of the Reserve parts of Barnegat Bay and the barrier islands on the east, Delaware Bay to the south, and the Maurice River on the west. The northwestern boundary follows several highways. Thus, what was once called the "Pine Barrens" is different from the region today called the "Pinelands."

The environmental remapping coincided with a new approach to the region and its people by cultural researchers, one which regarded the aquifer as a unifying feature. Folklorist Mary Hufford, planner Jonathan Berger, and historian John W. Sinton, all of whom did seminal work in documenting the people of the Pinelands and their use of the land, defined the region by the interrelationships of groups and traditional activities, and emphasized the insider's point of view in descriptions of the region.

In 1983, when the American Folklife Center at the Library of Congress established the Pinelands Folklife Project under Hufford's direction, fieldworkers surveyed all the traditional activities of people throughout the Reserve, concentrating particularly on their interactions with the environment. In addition to folklorists, members of the research team included an environmental psychologist and an ethnobotanist; this underscored the importance to the project of documenting the perceptions and understandings that constitute a group's sense of place and that underlie regional folklife.

During the same period, Berger and Sinton were studying the culture of people throughout the Reserve to assist in the creation of a management plan which would be informed by the needs of traditional users. In their book, *Water, Earth, and Fire: Land Use and Environmental Planning in the New Jersey Pine Barrens,* they describe the people of the Pinelands as " . . . no

Cranberry scoop made by Dan Aker at Giberson's Mill. New Jersey State Museum Collection, 174.51. Photograph by Joseph Crilley.

more isolated, nor . . . startlingly different, from rural cultures in other mid-Atlantic sections. They share with other rural people common values, including love of place, the central role of the family, Christian morality, participation in seasonal activities (farming, hunting, trapping) and participation in voluntary organizations (civic organizations, fire companies)."[11]

Hufford, Berger, and Sinton documented the ways in which natives perceive their place and build their lives with that knowledge. Their analyses of these perceptions begin this story of the Pinelands.

Mary T. Hufford first explains how sense of place "literally begins with the senses." She describes how sensory familiarity is a basis for concepts of place that are expressed in folklife forms. Through these forms, residents both organize and tell about their knowledge of the place.

John W. Sinton's essay then traces the broad history of human use of the Pinelands and describes the regional patterns of continuity and change. He explains how human activities created the present landscape.

In the concluding essay by Rita Moonsammy, David S. Cohen, and Mary T. Hufford, traditional activities within each of five major environmental subsystems of the Pinelands are described in historical sequence. Details of folk technologies are added to Sinton's framework of resource use, and descriptions of folklife forms and the perceptions of natives illustrate Hufford's analysis of "sense of place." Wherever possible, the words of residents are used, from both historical sources such as diaries and letters and contemporary sources such as interviews conducted during the Pinelands Folklife Project.

Through these analyses and descriptions, the remarkable variety of the place and its people, and the important folklife forms that link them, will enrich the story of the Pinelands.

NOTES

1. Ecological material for this essay has been provided by Beryl Robichaud and was drawn from her previous work. See Beryl Robichaud and Emily Russell, *Protecting the New Jersey* *Pinelands: The First National Reserve,* forthcoming, and Beryl Robichaud, *A Conceptual Framework for Pinelands Decision-Making* (New Brunswick, NJ: Center for Coastal and Environmental

Studies, Rutgers University, 1980). Portions of the latter were directly incorporated in Chapters 2 and 3 of the Comprehensive Management Plan for the Pinelands Commission in 1980.

2. Ives Goddard, "Delaware," in *Handbook of North American Indians*, ed. William C. Sturtevant, vol. 15, *Northeast*, ed. Bruce G. Trigger (Washington, DC: Smithsonian Institution, 1978), 213–239; and Herbert C. Kraft and R. Alan Mounier, "The Late Woodland Period in New Jersey: ca. A.D. 1000–1600," in *New Jersey's Archaeological Resources from the Paleo-Indian Period to the Present*, ed. Olga Chesler (Trenton: New Jersey Department of Environmental Protection, 1982), 139–184.

3. Samuel Smith, *History of the Colony of Nova-Caesaria, or New Jersey: Containing An Account of its First Settlement, Progressive Improvements, the Original and Present Constitution, and Other Events, to the Year 1721. With Some Particulars Since; and a Short View of its Present State.* (Burlington, NJ: James Parker, 1765), 487–488.

4. David J. Fowler, "Nature Stark Naked: A Social History of the New Jersey Seacoast and Pine Barrens, 1690–1800" (Ph.D. dissertation proposal, Rutgers University, 1981), 3–6.

5. David Steven Cohen, "The Origin of the 'Pineys': Local Historians and the Legend," *Folklife Annual* I (1985): 40–59.

6. Henry Herbert Goddard, *The Kallikak Family: A Study in the Heredity of Feeble-Mindedness* (New York: The Macmillan Company, 1913).

7. J. David Smith, *Minds Made Feeble: The Myth and Legacy of the Kallikaks* (Rockville, MD: Aspen, 1985).

8. Herbert Norman Halpert, "Folktales and Legends from the New Jersey Pines: A Collection and a Study" (Ph.D. dissertation, Indiana University, 1947); "Piney Folk Singers: Interviews, Photos, and Songs," *Direction* 2 (1939): 4–6, 15; "Some Ballads and Folk Songs from New Jersey," *Journal of American Folklore* 52 (1939): 52–69.

9. John McPhee, *The Pine Barrens* (New York: Farrar, Straus, and Giroux, 1968), 5.

10. Ibid., 13–14.

11. Jonathan Berger and John W. Sinton, *Water, Earth, and Fire: Land Use and Environmental Planning in the New Jersey Pine Barrens* (Baltimore: Johns Hopkins University Press, 1985), 11, 13.

JOE'S PLACE
AFTER DARK
TRESPASSERS
WILL BE SHOT
SURVIVORS
WILL BE PROSECUTED
PLEASE
NOVISITING
AFTERDARK
JOE

TELLING THE LANDSCAPE:

Folklife Expressions and Sense of Place

"I THINK OF TWO LANDSCAPES," WRITES BARRY LOPEZ, "ONE outside the self, the other within."

The external landscape is the one we see—not only the line and color of the land and its shading at different times of the day, but also its plants and animals in season, its weather, its geology, the record of its climate and evolution. . . . The second landscape I think of is an interior one, a kind of projection within a person of a part of the exterior landscape. . . . The interior landscape responds to the character and subtlety of the exterior one; the shape of the individual mind is affected by land as it is by genes.[1]

Connecting the outer and inner landscapes are landscape tellings. The word "telling" operates on several levels. In one sense, telling alludes to the way in which Pinelands residents take stock of landscape elements, assigning them values and names. They study the environment to tell what is there, perceiving differences in surroundings that at first seem indecipherable. This environmental literacy, the ability to read the environment, relies upon the accuracy of the environmental image, a collaborative vision of a given place that guides people who must constantly make their way through it, and who have for generations shaped it into what we see today.

Mary T. Hufford

Opposite: Woodland signpost on the road to Joe Albert's cabin. Forked River Mountains, Waretown. Photograph by Mary Hufford.

13

In the sense that telling also applies to the act of recounting or narrating, people constantly interpret the landscapes they have mentally ordered. Their interpretations crystallize in expressive forms that fuse and transform both inner and outer landscapes—songs, names for things, paintings, recipes, rituals, and tools and technologies for working the land. Such forms and processes contain stories—telling us the elements of the landscape and then telling its story through folklife.

The living landscape is hard to pick out at first. Before it was molded, it was deciphered into categorical forms, the "pieces" discerned and ordered into backdrops for human action on the land. These distinctions are indiscernible to the motorist passing through miles of ground oak and scrub pine, a landscape that folklorist Herbert Halpert described in the 1940s as "desolate and dreary":

> In many places one can travel for miles on the through highways with no relief from the uniform bleakness save for infrequent gas stations or narrow sand roads leading off to someone's bog. Houses are few and far between, gray and weatherbeaten, in marked contrast to the well-painted structures of the surrounding farm country. The house usually rests on what seems to be pure sand, and the scrub pine comes up almost to the doorstep.[2]

For Merce Ridgway, Sr., a woodsman who made charcoal early in this century near Bamber, such a landscape was enlivened with family and occupational history. When he moved to the Shore to make his living as a bayman, he nostalgically remembered the woods in "The Pine Barrens Song":

> I left the place where I was born, many years ago.
> For times were tough and work was scarce,
> I had no choice but go.
> But I've been back there many a time, in my memory,
> Of all the places that I've been, it's there I'd rather be—
>
> Where the scrub pine, ground oak, berry bush, and sand,
> They never changed—they never will—Pine Barrens land—
> The sweet May pink and curly fern, leaves all turning green,
> And the water running red in the cedar swamp stream.[3]

Ridgway's song also records other facets of the backdrop against which woodsmen perform—sand roads through twisted pine trees, cemeteries, the smell of pine smoke from wood stoves, and ruins of towns left by failed industries. The landscape he describes is as man-made as it is natural. Humans have carved it into roads, ditches, channels, fields, settlements, and banks, and it has etched its features into the collective memory.

The song provides a short list of plants that are significant to woodsmen—evoking an impression of what the place looks and smells like. Scrub pine, ground oak, berry bushes and sand are ubiquitous, both sources of income and indicators that tell about the environment. They are scenic resources in the theatrical sense that J. B. Jackson reminds us of:

When we speak of the "scenes of our childhood," or borrow Pope's phrase and refer to the world as "this scene of man," we are using the word *scene* in what seems a literal sense: as meaning location, the place where something happens. It rarely occurs to us that we have in fact borrowed a word from the theater to use as a metaphor. Yet originally *scene* meant stage, as it still does in French, and when it first became common in everyday speech it still suggested its origin: the world (we were implying) was a theater, and we were at once actors and audience.[4]

The actors and audiences read their cues in the natural settings. The colors of serotinous (delayed-opening) pine cones reveal how long it has been since a fire has occurred; an abundance or dearth of acorns may disclose feeding patterns of deer; vegetation indicates the kind of "bottom" (substrate) on which it grows; and in the sand woodsmen can read what animals have passed through recently (they can even identify fellow woodsmen by distinctive tire tracks). May pinks, as trailing arbutus is called locally, are a welcome sign of spring. The curly fern Ridgway mentions is not *Schizea pusilla*, a tiny, relict plant that environmentalists point to as a regional symbol, but rather the large bracken ferns (*Pteridium aquilinum*) that Koreans gather and consume in the spring. Ridgway's nostalgic portrait, painted from memory, is meaningful to people whose interior landscapes resemble his.

Outsiders to the Pinelands often marvel at the perceptive skills of natives, as Captain Lou Peterson, a Delaware Bay oysterman, observed to Jens Lund:

I don't think that you consciously know anything. I think living around this area and growin' up around it, your senses become used to it or somethin', because, you take my father-in-law, he moved down in 1950, and he couldn't get over the fact that every native down here, when the wind changed, noticed it.[5]

Sense of place literally begins with the senses, with an ability to make sense of the environment, not only to tell what is there, but to understand the relationships between environmental elements. Outdoorsmen working in what we might call the endemic folklife habitats of the Pinelands may or may not express ecological relationships in scientific terms, but they know what the place looks, sounds, tastes, smells, and feels like at different times of the day and in different seasons. Environmental literacy is for them a survival skill that enables them to "work the cycle."

The high sensitivity to wind is important not only for watermen but also for woodsmen, who contend with the dangers of living near fire-climax forests. Awareness of the imminence of fire—the ability to read what Jack Cervetto, a Warren Grove woodsman, calls the "fire index"—is widespread among natives. "The old timers always knew to check the fire index," Cervetto observed. "Young people don't seem to check for it so much any more." The buildup of pine needles and brush on sandy soil that holds no water creates a tinder-box. Natives are tensed when a fire is overdue, like people elsewhere, who, living on the margins of disaster, are tensed for volcanic eruptions, or earthquakes, or floods. "When she's ready to burn," wrote Joanne Van Istendal, of Medford, "the wind will dry her like a bone. You gotta feel and smell the wind, be ready for a good fight. When there's a fire at the other end of the Pines, we all feel it. It's always on our minds. It binds us together."[6]

Herbert Payne, who made charcoal in Whiting, was able to "tend" his charcoal pit from his job on a construction site many miles away in Toms River. One day, noticing a sudden shift in the wind, he excused himself to the foreman and hurried home, arriving just in time to keep the charcoal from completely combusting.[7]

Woodsmen, in turn, marvel at the perceptual acuities of animals, who they may regard as teachers, rivals, saboteurs, companions, and assistants. "We're a class of animal, too," reflected Harry Payne, "a higher class of animal." He spoke admiringly of the acute senses that make foxes so hard to trap, and that enable birds to "forecast the weather":

They know an awful lot, to keep away from the human being—because naturally we're smarter than they are to a degree, but I think they're more sensible to nature than we are. They can forecast the weather, they know when there's going to be a storm. You can tell by the way they move. In the afternoon you'll see a little cloud in the sky and you'll see the birds goin' way up high and comin' down, keep goin' way up high and flutterin'—you know there's gonna be a storm that afternoon—a hard thunderstorm.[8]

The trapper, as folklorist Gerald Parsons reminds us, has an extremely fine-grained image of the world:

> In the vastness of a tide marsh, he looks for the track of a mink no larger than a thumb-print. Where the fin-fisherman watches for the flash of bait fish on the surface of the ocean, or looks across the broad horizon to find a cloud of feeding sea birds, the trapper searches the ground under his boots for the glint of a few dried fish scales—otter vomit.[9]

Fur traders, botanists, herpetologists, deer hunters, and horticulturists have relied upon the senses of local woodsmen–gatherers for generations, for they have powers of discernment that seem astonishing. The historian Harold Wilson tells us that woodsmen who mined cedar near Dennisville in the early nineteenth century "progged" for the ancient fallen trees with rods in the swamps. (People who wrest their livings from the muck are, in fact, known as "proggers.") There were two kinds of trees: "windfalls," which had toppled with their roots attached, and "breakdowns," which had broken off. Wilson reports that because breakdowns were more easily mined, a log digger would first secure a chip from any log he discovered, determining by the smell of the chip whether the tree was a windfall or a breakdown.[10]

A keen sense of smell is still important to woodsmen. Tom Brown, a woodsman from Cumberland County, may avoid a place that smells like cucumbers, a sure sign that rattlesnakes are nearby: "I've been blueberrying with the wife and I said, 'Come on, let's get out of here!' She said, 'Why?' 'Let's go! Cause I *smell* 'em!' They got that odor, you know—like fresh-cut cucumbers."[11]

Elizabeth White and Frederick Coville developed the world's first culti-

Five-eighths inch gauge to measure wild blueberries used by Elizabeth White and Frederick Coville. Drawing by Allen Carroll. Based on aluminum replica by Mark Darlington.

vated blueberries at Whitesbog in the early 1900s. They were aided by woodsmen—gatherers who, it was said, could almost navigate by the tastes of blueberries in different swamps, and by their shapes and sizes. Attempting to develop a cultivated strain from the wild blueberries, White enlisted the woodsmen in her search for bushes bearing the largest berries. She devised a pay scale for bushes bearing fruit that would not fall through the $\frac{5}{8}$-inch hole in her blueberry gauge, and she named the bushes after their finders:

> In getting the early bushes I tried to name every bush after the finder. . . . And so I had the Adams bush found by Jim Adams, the Harding bush that was found by Ralph Harding, and the Dunphy bush that was found by Theodore Dunphy. When Sam Lemmon found a bush I could not name it the Lemmon bush, so I called it the Sam. Finally, Rube Leek of Chatsworth found a bush. I did not know it was anything special at that time, and I used the full name in my notes. . . . Coville called it the Rube, which I thought was a poor name for an aristocratic bush. He finally suggested that we call it the Rubel. And the Rubel has been the keystone of blueberry breeding.[12]

At the second annual Whitesbog Blueberry Festival, held in 1985 by the Whitesbog Preservation Trust, local children went on a blueberry hunt. Each child was equipped with a $\frac{5}{8}$-inch gauge made by Elizabeth White's great-nephew, Mark Darlington. They took their gauges into the old blueberry fields around Whitesbog to find the biggest berries. The winner received a flat of cultivated blueberries. Thus, in a bit of historic re-enactment, the relationship between the horticulturists and woodsman—gatherers that produced the cultivated blueberry is commemorated.

The effort to achieve contact with nature and contact with the past is often formalized in such recreational activities. Aldo Leopold observes that a key aesthetic feature of nature contact is "the perception of evolutionary and/or ecological processes."[13] Activities such as blueberry games, deer hunting, and birding formalize the challenge of reading natural "texts," a challenge met by those who first tamed the wilderness.

"Have you ever followed a deer trail?" asked one deer hunter from the Spartan Gun Club:

> You have to be able to read signs to know what's goin' on—you find droppings, you find their beds, you find buck rubs, which are young saplings that they rub the bark off when they take the fuzz off their antlers, and

these young saplings—about an inch and a half in diameter—these young saplings are all stripped of bark about that high off the ground where they slip the head down and get the fuzz off their antlers. They polish 'em up, get 'em ready for fightin' for a mate.[14]

Deer hunters see part of their mission as commemorative. Their annual re-enactments of the frontier days typify what Aldo Leopold termed "the split-rail fence" approach to recreation. "We have a saying," said Larry Carpenter, of the Harmony Gun Club, " 'Take your boy hunting instead of hunting your boy.' It *is* a tradition. . . . It's like American heritage. We take time off of work to come up and put in the time. We keep the population under control. Everything we take we use. It's just like what happened in the eighteenth century."[15]

Jim Stasz, an avid birder from Audubon, New Jersey (where John James Audubon, "the great American woodsman," once collected a scissor-tailed flycatcher), spoke of "reading" with one's eyes closed, using only one's ears and nose: "You could close your eyes, and listen to the birds and know what plants were there. Or you could look at the plants, even just smell them at certain seasons and you could predict what birds would be there."[16]

The Christmas Bird Count is an annual event of no less significance than deer hunting, a ritual celebration that occurs at the time of year when it is most challenging to find birds. This heightens the significance of what the participants are able to report afterwards, when the birders gather to tell of their discoveries.[17]

Franz Boas wrote that "all human activities may assume forms that give them esthetic values."[18] In a similar vein, folklorist Dell Hymes commented that all communities encapsulate shared experiences in "meaningful, apposite forms."[19]

These forms include all things that are crafted out of the imagination's encounter with the land and its resources—recipes, songs, poems, paintings, crafts, tools, technological processes, rituals, festivals, recreational activities, and landscapes. They show how communities organize both natural and cultural differences, and they serve as repositories of information about both nature and society—archives for the collective memory.

Information about the landscape, its places and people, its economic and seasonal cycles, its past, and its multiple realities, is encapsulated in the names for things within it. The following informal nomenclature for Pinelands groups suggests that people, like natural resources, may be classified as ecotypes: mudwallopers, pineys, stumpjumpers, proggers, river rats, snakehunters, baymen, and woodsmen. Even terms such as "transplant," for newcomers, and "shoobee," for tourists (who wear their shoes to the beach), address the referent's degree of removal from the land.

"The very naming and distinguishing of the environment," writes Kevin Lynch, "vivifies it, and thereby adds to the depth and poetry of human existence."[20]

Consider the three categories of names for plants: botanical names— Latin binomials conferred by an international congress of botanists; common names—"specific vernacular names selected by a regional body as the preferred non-botanical name for specific kinds of plants";[21] vernacular names—the local unstandardized names that show great geographical and cultural variation. "May pinks," for example, is a local name for *Epigea repens*, which goes by the common name of "trailing arbutus." The botanical, or scientific, names provide "knowledge about" natural species, identifying them in the format and language of an international classification system, and for the use of an international community of scientists. Local names, on the other hand, encapsulate human experience with the species on this landscape, conveying that "knowledge of" the place that is born of repeated experience with it.[22]

Scientific names often memorialize people relating to the history of an international community. The roster of scientific names for plants and reptiles reads like a roll call for botanists and zoologists. Pickering's morning glory (*Breweri pickeringi*), Fowler's toad (*Bufo woodhousei fowleri*), Knieskern's beakrush (*Rhynchospora knieskernii*), and Hirst's panic grass (*Panicum hirstii*). Peter Kalm and Mark Catesby, natural historians of the eighteenth century, are commemorated in the scientific names for sheep laurel (*Kalmia angustifolia*) and bullfrogs (*Rana catesbiana*).

Local names for plants and animals, however, spring from experience with a place. Taken as a whole, they graphically catalog its sights, tastes, sounds, smells, and impressions: "sugar huck" (*Vaccinium vacillans*) is the sweetest wild huckleberry; "whompers" (*Lampropeltus gitulis gitulis*) are immense eastern king snakes that live in the swamps; "green juggers" (*Rana catesbiana*) are bullfrogs; "stinkpots" (*Sternotherus odoratus*) are turtles, so named, according to Tom Brown, because they urinate on people who pick them up; "squawks" (*Nicticorax nicticorax*) are black-crowned night-herons, so named, according to Bill Lee, for their raucous calls; "croakers" (*Micropogonias undulatus*) and "drumfish" (*Pogonias cromis*) fill the bay with their "singing," as Bill Lee put it; "puff adders" (*Heterodon platyrhinos*) inflate themselves and play dead when disturbed; "snappers" (*Chelydra serpentina*) command respect for their jaws; "rattlers" (*Crotalus horridus*) issue percussive warnings; and "woodjin's enemy" (*Comptonia asplenifolia*) is sweet-fern, laden with the sand-ticks so bothersome to "woodjins"—a portmanteau word combining "woodsman" and "Injun."

Blueberries and huckleberries continue to go by practical names. Local names for the wild berries include "upland blacks" (*Gaylussacia dumosa*), also called "grouseberries" (Marucci), "grassberries," and "dwarf hucks" (Harshberger); "black huckleberries" (*Gaylussacia resinosa*); "swamp black" (*Vaccinium attrococcum*); "sugar hucks" (*Vaccinium vacillans*); and "dangleberries" or "bilberries" (*Gaylussacia frondosa*). "There's three different types, and three different sizes of blue huckleberries," said Jack Cervetto, a Warren Grove woodsman, "Now the swamp blues (*Vaccinium corymbosum*), now they're the largest and the best ones for pie. I have cultivated berries at home, but I'll go in the swamp and get blues if my wife wants to make a pie."[23]

The environmental image, on which outdoorsmen must agree in order to communicate, is condensed in names and in other folklife expressions, many of which serve as mnemonic forms that keep the region's collective memory accessible.

"The named environment," writes Kevin Lynch, "familiar to all, furnishes material for common memories and symbols which bind the group together and allow them to communicate with one another. The landscape serves as a vast mnemonic system for the retention of group history and ideals."[24]

Local people often describe wild phenomena through domestic analogues. Tiny cedar saplings come up, said George Brewer, "like hair on a dog's back." Elizabeth Woodford compared the sound of a controlled burn to "bacon crackling in a skillet." Tom Brown likens the odor of rattlesnakes to cucumbers, and Jack Cervetto thinks of sphagnum moss as a rug. It smells, he says, "like iodine." Brad Thompson sees the Inner and Outer Coastal Plains coming together "like fingers in a line," where husbanded soil and virgin soil may be read in the alternating fields of soybeans and blueberries. Croakers, drumfish, and weakfish fill the bay with their "singing," according to Bill Lee. Hunters distinguish the two species of foxes by placing red foxes in the dog family, and gray foxes in the cat family.

Place names, linked with landscape features, encode the shared past, distinguishing members of one group from another. "Let me show you where I was born," said Richard Gille, the zoning officer for Lacey Township:

There's a foundation there where I was born, and when I was a kid, the train used to stop here to pick up water, and there was a small little stop house—there wasn't actually a station. We called that Ostrum. But only somebody like me or Johnny Parker or Cliff Frazee would know if I said "Ostrum" that I was talkin' about that. That was right along the railroad. The train that ran there was steam and they had to pick up the water there. So they called that part of town Ostrum, and when I was a kid, we said we didn't live in Forked River, we lived in Ostrum.[25]

The charred remains of an event in natural history may also become a nucleus around which common memories are gathered. Lacking the touchstones to the past that ruins of settlements provide, places in the woods are more subtle, defined by the people and events that coalesce in them. "Webby was great for naming places," said Jack Davis, "Clarence Webb. He's the one come out with 'Lightnin' Point,' 'cause of this tree that was hit with lightnin'. That's known as Lightnin' Point nowadays by the older people."[26] One space may be several places at once, reflected in the names given to it by its various users. Near Woodmansie is a place that the older local people call "The Clay Pits." The lakes left there by an extractive industry are now called "Hidden Lakes" by the recreational-vehicle users who swarm there each weekend from points as far as 50 miles away.

Places and their names are sources of identity and security. Joe Albert, an octogenarian woodsman from Waretown, was frustrated in his effort to formally designate a favorite woodland crossroads:

The main corner up here by the fire tower, I named that Star Tree Corner—it's like a star. I always keep paintin' signs and nailin' 'em up there, and guys steals 'em! . . . I put it there so it'd keep that name, you know—the younger ones don't follow things up like that. Now they tell me that sign is down by a little camp on the hill.[27]

Wilderness-seekers might be startled by signs in the woods. Yet these seekers are themselves partly defined as a community by their own shared system of place names. "Do you have names for the sections you hunt?" I asked a member of the Spartan Gun Club in Chatsworth. He was incredulous. "How can you name anything like that? It's in the woods!" Yet, as it turned out, they did have names for places:

"You know, you might have like the Double Dirt Road or Big Hill or Sandy Ridge. . . ."
"Down by the Crooked Tree. . . ."
"Two or three deadfall trees together: 'Down by the Big Deadfall,' 'Sandy Ridge,' or 'Apple Pie Hill.'"[28]

Children living in Pinelands communities play at frontiering, building "forts" in the woods, as children have done for at least half a century. Their worlds are not as large, but they are as diversified as adult woodlands, which the children may regard as threatening. Frank Day, 13, of Lebanon Lakes, identified Hidden Lakes as a scary place: "The kids said all these guys go back there and chase them. . . . Probably Pineys. Hunters—wild hunters."[29] The children's landmarks are "The Old Pine Tree" or "The Rotten Out Tree"—a tree with a hole in it that squirrels live in.

Like tides with place names bobbing in them, successive generations wash over the region, and sometimes the names stick—serving, like the advice of older people, as landmarks for future generations.

It is difficult to consider the landscape apart from folklife expressions, because the landscape itself is partly the work of human hands. It has been so extensively modified that its crafted aspects are an integral part of it.

"This is a high ridge here," said Nora Rubinstein to Jack Cervetto, standing on a raised area near an old cranberry bog.

"This is a dam," Jack corrected her. "This is man-made. This is built."

What appear to be monotonous woodlands to outsiders are teeming with categorical forms in the eyes of woodsmen.

"All right," said Jack Cervetto to Nora Rubinstein, "Now see that water we just went through? That separates that island from this island. Now this is another island surrounded by water."

"How can you tell that it's a slough and not just a wet spot?" Nora inquired.

"Well, it's low all the way around it. Altogether different bottom. . . . Last week this was perfectly dry. The rain we had the other day has put some water in here."

"Does this island have a name?"

"No, no. But it's my island, and I'm pretty well attached to it."[30]

"Islands," "sloughs," and "bottom" are landscape motifs, grammatical units in the language of those who read the environment. These units may be natural entities that are mentally discerned and endowed with meaning, or they may be human constructions with historic legacies, such as channels, ditches, dams, bogs, sand roads, corduroy roads, and charcoal pits.

The old corduroy roads or crossways that criss-cross the swamps contain lessons about the old-timers' ways of harvesting and managing cedar. They are blueprints for the new roads, as Clifford Frazee observed:

> The old timers did it that way. We put the brush on the crossway, and that holds the slabs in position. We leave the slabs right there and the

cedar won't reseed in the road, and the trees'll grow up on both sides and meet at the top. I can show you a couple of places where it was cut off like a hundred years ago. It's rotted out, but the trees don't grow up in it. The advantage is that it gives a tree five extra feet for growth. You should thin out cedar, but if you thin it too much the wind'll blow it over. We fall 'em toward the crossway, and most of 'em fall right on it. You have to notch 'em just right to have 'em fall.[31]

Puerto Rican Sacred Heart altar, home of Eugene Espinosa of Lakewood. Photograph by Dennis McDonald. New Jersey State Council on the Arts.

Walking on such a crossway conveys Frazee into the swamp, into the past, and into a reflection on the most critical problem in cedar management: striking a balance between sunlight, which makes the trees grow faster, and crowding, which keeps out the sun, but protects the trees against windthrow.

Long-time residents can often critically appraise the landscape, and appreciate subtle nuances relevant to traditions in which they have been trained. Norman Taylor, on returning to the site of his childhood home in Lower Mill after 20 years, excitedly witnessed in retrospect his father's good judgment in locating the mill at the confluence of two streams: "You can see why it's appropriate for a mill to be there, where two streams come together—look how quick the water is. . . . You can see the piling down there where the old mill used to set. That's a lot of water flowing, for as low as the water is."[32]

Farmers enjoy looking at farms that look as farms should look. For them, farms are critical scenic resources. "It's a pretty, pretty sight," said Mary Lamonaca, a peach grower in Hammonton, "when the fruit is in bloom, when the fruit is hanging, the tomato fields, and the beautiful rows of baskets."[33]

"Every orchard and every field has its own different thing, see?" said Eddie Lamonaca, her husband, showing his farming community to Mal O'Connor: "Now coming up here, you've got . . . Pine Road, a pretty nice road, you know. . . . Most of it's kept well around here. There's nothing shabby or rundown about the farms. They're meticulous."[34] The trained landscape observer knows when to applaud technical skill, and exhibitions of what Franz Boas called "feeling for form,"—whether the crafted work is a cranberry bog, a Maryland hound dog, or a Barnegat Bay sneakbox.

Folklife expressions help to keep people oriented in the face of drastic cultural change. When communities or individuals are separated from their cultural contexts, they may encapsulate that lost world in some form, using the materials at hand as touchstones that confirm their own sources. Thus, for example, Lydia Gonzalez told Bonnie Blair that Puerto Ricans in

The Last Supper, *framed by deer antlers, and snapping turtle shell painted with a duck scene. Tom Brown's trapper cabin, Millville. Photograph by Joseph Czarnecki. PFP83–B217721–14–8.*

Woodbine "don't lose themselves," because they keep their houses "the old way, with their Sagrado Corazon [Sacred Heart] and their plastic flowers and everything, and still really cook the old way all the time."[35]

Religion and foodways—resources for spiritual and physical nourishment—are common foci for communal identity. People bind themselves to the "great traditions" of Judaism and Christianity with the "little traditions" of their own design.[36] Copies of Da Vinci's *The Last Supper,* for example, are framed differently in different cultural settings. In Valia Petrenko's Russian Orthodox home, the scene is draped with a *rushnyk* (a traditional embroidered towel), while in Tom Brown's trapper's cabin it is flanked by two deer antlers; thus, reminders of Russian culture and South Jersey nature, respectively, are linked through a painting that bridges and articulates cultural difference.

Food is an important focus of communal identity for both long-established natives and more recently arrived immigrants. "I don't lose my way of doing things," said Clara Paolino of Ancora, speaking of her ability

The Last Supper, *framed by Russian* rushnyk *(ceremonial cloth), home of Valia Petrenko, Allentown. Photograph by Dennis McDonald. New Jersey State Council on the Arts.*

to produce a wide range of Italian dishes out of the gardens of relatives and neighbors.[37] Ann Davis, of Brown's Mills, spoke of the Piney way to make snapper soup:

> I shred my snapper. I start out with cabbage, potatoes, celery, onions, carrots—cooked in stock. Then string beans, peas, whatever you want. Then I put six pounds of butter. Then . . . hard boiled eggs that I ground. That's the Piney way that we make snapper soup. In restaurants you get that brown gravy soup, and I don't like it.[38]

People "read" people by the ways they do things, just as they read the environment. Some people claim to be able to tell a New Gretna speaker from a Green Bank speaker. Decoy aficionados distinguish subregional styles among carvers—the Parkertown style, the New Gretna style, the "Head of the Bay" style, and the Tuckerton style.

Even stylistic differences in oyster shucking methods mark different re-

Peach orchard, Hammonton. Photograph by Joseph Czarnecki. PFP217721—4—4.

gional backgrounds. People from Virginia are accustomed to the long, thin oysters called "hotdogs" or "snaps" in southern Maryland.[39] They "break" their oysters open by smashing the shell. People from Maryland learn to open oysters that are shorter and rounder, and separate the two shells by "stabbing" the knife between them. When people from Maryland and Virginia converged in the same shucking houses in Port Norris they were quickly differentiated into "breakers" and "stabbers." "I'd want my back to the breaker," said Beryl Whittington, who stabs his oysters "straight out," "because the breaker throws a lot more mud. Sometimes the shell from a breaker will pop you upside the head."[40]

Certain landscape elements may reflect transplanted ethnic values. "The topography is always 'trying' to match an image," wrote Paul Shepard. "This meshing brings order out of the natural world without homogenizing it."[41] Many of the farms surrounding Hammonton, for example, are Italian, as the names on the mailboxes attest: DeMarco, Risotti, Putiri, Angelo, Bucci, Lamonaca. They also *look* Italian, according to Eddie Lamonaca: "Italian farmers, I think, like to see trees, and olive trees, or peach trees. . . . Some kind of a gnarly, European-growing-looking tree—and the ground's flat, you know, and has some kind of rolling landscape to it. . . . I think it does resemble Italy somewhat—northern Italy, and central Italy."[42]

For the same reason, Russian and Ukrainian immigrants in Cassville line their yards with colonnades of white birch trees transplanted from local bogs. Reminiscent of Eastern European forests, birch trees powerfully evoke the homeland.

The remains of some of the Pinelands National Reserve's fragile landscapes are just as symbolically powerful. For George Campbell, a fourth-generation salt-hay farmer, the man-made banks that have maintained the meadows represent a way of life that is being consumed by the ocean: "Last year I was down on my bay shore down here. My bank had broke, you know. I stood there and cried 'cause I seen a way of life leavin', you know, that I'd loved, and you can only fight Mother Nature for so long and she's gonna win. I know she's gonna win."[43]

Many technological processes in the Pinelands aspire toward the most precise balance possible between beauty and efficiency. When they achieve that balance, they are likely to be considered an art form, as Franz Boas observed:

> When the technical treatment has attained a certain standard of excellence, when the control of the processes involved is such that certain typical forms are produced, we call the process an art, and however simple the forms may be, they may be judged from the point of view of formal perfection; industrial pursuits such as cutting, carving, moulding, weaving; as well as singing, dancing and cooking are capable of attaining technical excellence and fixed forms.[44]

"Now that's an art in itself, building a corduroy road," said George Brewer, who harvests cedar in Great Cedar Swamp. The list of forms and processes accorded this status in the Pinelands is lengthy. Processes such as trapping, canning, farming, net making, boatbuilding, eeling, fox hunting, bog building, glassblowing, and lumbering all have aesthetic as well as pragmatic aspects, laden with personal and communal significance. Out of them emerge emblems of regional identity—Jersey cedar, Jersey cones, Jersey tomatoes, and Jersey garveys.

Created at the intersection of the inner and outer landscapes described by Barry Lopez are the tools for plying the exterior landscape, many of which attained fixed forms generations ago. The body of maritime tools yields a remarkably complete image of the waterman's workplace in its varied aspects at different seasons. Tools for clamming, oystering, and eeling, for example, reflect the varied nuances of "bottom"—some geological, some seasonal—below the region's diverse waters. There are, for example, eel spears for summer and winter, and at least three different kinds of heads for clam and oyster tongs: wooden, barrel, and keyport. Wooden heads are made of seasoned oak, with teeth of sawed-off steel pounded through; they are the best for soft bottom. "You can catch oysters with wooden heads when you can't catch anything but mud with the other ones," said Lou Peterson to Jens Lund. "You have to feel your tongs, and hold up on them, and you can pretty near feel the oysters goin' in."[45]

Such tools, like stories, are eloquent interpretations of the environment that may reflect the personalities of their makers and users. Rube Corlies' black-duck decoys, for example, are unmistakable, because of his effort to keep them ice-free:

> . . . Rube's ducks are high on the front, tufted breast from the bottom to the bill and the reason he made 'em that high was because in a blow, when the wind is blowing and your duck is dipping, and the temperature is falling, that bill will hit the water and it'll start to ice up, and the

Black-duck decoy made by Ruben Corlies (1882–1976) of Manahawkin. Drawing by Allen Carroll.

first thing you know you got an icicle about that long on the duck's bill. So as long as he could keep 'em high and keep 'em out of the water, he'd keep 'em from icing up just that much longer.[46]

In recent decades, collectors have recognized the aesthetic value of such decoys, but as Ted Von Bosse, of Port Republic, pointed out, such artistry was incidental to their main function. "They made them to hunt with, not as art, but there's art in those things, and there's shape and beauty in the old ducks that's just beyond belief."[47]

The artistry in duck hunting does not begin and end with hand-carved decoys, however. Whether he uses cedar, cork, or plastic decoys, the skill of the duck hunter resides in his ability to perceive and exploit a variety of factors, including wind direction, temperature, tide, and his position relative to the ducks. His goal is to create an impression with his decoys that will attract flying ducks within shooting range. Ed Hazelton's brother-in-law was a good duck hunter, according to Ed, because he thought like his quarry:

> He was the type of fella that thought like a duck. He thought like a duck. He just knew every move they were gonna make. In other words, we'd sit there, gunning, and have the stools [decoys] out, and in would come some ducks. And they wouldn't come just the way he wanted 'em. Just exactly right. You *could* kill 'em, but he says, "They gotta do better than that." And he would go out and he would take this stool here and put it there, and this stool here and set it back there, and the next time they'd almost light in your lap. . . . He just thought like a duck all the time. He knew . . . when there would be a lid on the bay . . . and that the ducks would come in to feed in the ponds before the freeze.[48]

These are the aesthetic judgments, the critical canons that guide the development of forms. Each practitioner contributes to the form in the way that scholars contribute to their own disciplines. We see this especially in the indigenous small watercraft of the Pinelands.

"There are two kinds of garvey makers," says Ed Hazelton, "builders, and craftsmen." A builder, inattentive to details, might produce a "hairy" garvey—one that is unsanded, and comes out looking "like a crew cut" beneath its paint job. Also, a real craftsman, according to Hazelton, drills a hole for each nail to prevent cracks that eventually widen into leaks.[49]

The Barnegat Bay sneakbox, one of the most elegant forms to emerge from the region, effectively synthesizes the observations of generations of baymen of water, land, air, man, and mud. It was custom made for the marshes and estuaries of South Jersey. In its form we see every contingency neatly anticipated. Its spoon-shaped hull enables it to glide through areas marked as land on coastal maps. Only Atlantic white cedar will produce the requisite compound curves, according to builders George Heinrichs and John Chadwick, who use old family patterns. The tiny skiff—12 feet long by 4 feet amidships—is light enough for one man to haul over land between channels. It is equipped with a mast-hole, centerboard well, and detachable rudder for sailing; winter and summer sails; folding oarlocks and a removable decoy rack to suppress its profile; runners for traveling on ice; and two kinds of accessory ice hooks for breaking up slushy ("porridge") and hard ("pane") ice. Its sloping transom allows a hunter to row backward in channels that are too narrow to turn around in. It is linked in tradition with the Barnegat Bay duck stool, a decoy with a dugout (hollow-carved) body to lighten the boat's burden and keep its draft shallow enough, as the saying goes, "to follow a mule as it sweats up a dusty road."

In the sneakbox the shapes of men and meadows are fused. The planked-over deck, which keeps the gunner's legs warm, was often custom made. "They used to build a sneakbox special for a man," Sam Hunt once said. "He used to lay down on the ground and they'd draw a circle around him and build a hatch so his belly could stick out."[50]

The sneakbox incorporates many facets of the South Jersey environment—alluding in its design to independent gunners, cedar swamps, salt meadows, mud, water, ice, winter, summer, and wind.

Some tools and technologies, such as boats, decoys, corduroy roads, and orchards, are tangible creations—each instance of the form an enduring crystallization of environmental concepts. Others, such as decoy rigs, sets for catching fox and muskrat, and ways of casting nets for fish, are repeatedly produced and dismantled.

The ultimate harvest, however, is the story, captured through formalized pursuits, such as yardscaping, birding and hunting. We have seen how individuals formalize their perceptions of nature in narrative, songs, and paintings, and how Pinelands communities formalize nature contact in activities such as birding and deer, duck, and fox hunting. Such activities are wellsprings for stories that create the environmental image.

Hunting of any sort can provide a way to interact with wildlife, whether or not any game is taken. Ann Davis recalled her opportunities for witnessing wildlife dramas:

> My mother wouldn't understand why I wanted to go gunning. But I would go up into the woods and set there by myself, and listen to the squirrels cussing me out, and the blue jays, and you get in where they are, and they don't like you to interrupt what they're doing . . . and till they find you there they're just unconcerned, but when they find you, boy oh boy! You'd be surprised how they chatter, and the blue jays'll see you and they'll go up and down the woods and the road hollerin', and I said, "They're just tellin' everybody else that somebody's here." I believe that that's what it was. And a deer could come along, and the squirrels and the blue jays would tell him, "Don't go any further!" And off they would run. It's really amazing the things that you see and hear off in the woods.[51]

Fox hunting ceases in March when foxes begin raising their young, but foxes will still perform for those who know where to go, according to Norman Taylor:

> If you go out around April or May, and go where [the mother fox] has got little ones, she'll put on an act that is out of this world for you. She'll do everything in the world to get you away from that hole. She'll holler, she'll squawk, she'll let you see her, she'll run, she'll roll. She'll do anything to get you away from there.[52]

Such accounts view the landscape within a theatrical frame, a way of experiencing the landscape that differs from the scientific perspective. When we conceive of the landscape as an "ecosystem," we filter our image of it through a scientific analogue, an analogue that does not help us to fully appreciate the expressive dimension of the landscape. J. B. Jackson suggests that, in this regard, "theater" serves as a more useful metaphor, because, unlike ecosystem, it is drawn from human experience:

> All that we have so far come up with is an analogue of one sort or another, borrowed from biology or ecology or communication theory. When it is a matter of controlling or manipulating the environment, analogues can be extremely helpful; yet if we are again to learn how to respond emotionally and esthetically and morally to the landscape, we must find a metaphor—or several metaphors—drawn from our human experience.[53]

The landscapes of the Pinelands are indeed theatrical settings. Woodspeople scan them, focusing on the dramatic action, or "events," as Bill Wasiowich described them to John McPhee:

> When he is not working in the bogs, he goes roaming, as he puts it, setting out cross-country on long, looping journeys, hiking about thirty miles in a typical day, in search of what he calls "events"—surprising a buck, or a gray fox, or perhaps a poacher or a man with a still.[54]

Jack Cervetto's swamps are filled with natural dramas. Cedar trees, scraping against each other in the wind, make "music," while sphagnum moss repels mosquitoes with its iodine fumes. Against this backdrop he encounters the wildlife world, marveling at its strangeness, continually interpreting its mysteries. "The weirdest sound that I've heard in the swamp," he said, "is a snake swallowing a frog. It takes a long time for a snake to swallow a frog, and the whole time the frog is squeeching."[55]

"The green snake," he said, "They're the friendliest snake. . . . You approach that branch he'll stick his head out in front of you, but he won't bother you."

The biggest snake, the "whomper," is also called the "pilot" snake, according to Tom Brown, because tradition has it that it indicates where the rattlesnakes are.[56] "Have you seen a whomper?" Cervetto asked Eugene Hunn, "or heard 'em?"

> Oh, they're a big one. They're short, and great big, and boy, them sonofaguns, they're not afraid of anything. Now, my wife's uncle had charge of the Sim Place cranberry bog there—this oh, probably three years ago, and at night time us boys all hung around together there—Warren Grove, in the old candy store there. We used to play quoits and horseshoes and checkers and that, and he said, "Boys, I'm gonna show you somethin'." And he had one of these whompers. And this whomper had thirty-eight snakes inside of it, from twelve inches to eighteen inches long.[57]

While such natural events are not themselves works of art, they are, to borrow a concept from Robert Plant Armstrong, "affecting presences"[58] that move and amaze their witnesses. Nature is a wellspring of mysterious otherness, an "insistent and live reality," as David Wilson put it, present to its connoisseurs "the way God is to saints or the past is to humanists":

To come face to face with a flying spider or a rattlesnake in the road unhinges habit and intensifies awareness, just as stumbling upon an ancient rune does, or encountering a burning bush. These uncommon phenomena throw the settled world into disarray. . . . Close attention must be paid and care taken if one is to make sense of it all, and if the world is to make sense still. There are some who are dead to the impact of such events, but for those who are not, every detail seems significant and its gestalt feels compelling. It is like the difference between those who encounter a poem as an "affecting presence" and those who see it only as a batch of words.[59]

Tom Brown inventories his scenic resources in verse:

> My wife has often said to me,
> "How lonesome the woods must be,"
> I answered, "No, there's too much to see"—
> I love the murmur of the trees
> As the wind softly stirs her leaves
> The bees flying to and fro
> Gathering nectar as they go
> The robin and the little wren
> Among my many feathered friends
> The cardinal with his coat of red
> The mockingbird singing overhead
> At yonder log I chance to glance
> A grouse is starting to drum and dance
> The otter from the bank its slide
> The mink that hunts a hole to hide
> The deer that drink in yonder stream
> I often see them in my dreams
> And though folks may say it's a waste of time
> I'll always have this love of mine.[60]

Painters such as Margaret Bakely, of Vincentown, and the late Win Salmons, of New Gretna, have captured such natural events in paintings. Some scenes—deer browsing in a clearing, or ducks being flushed from the water—are common, and often appear on related flat surfaces produced by those environments, such as sand dollars and snapper shells. The kind of scene that would be virtually impossible to photograph, a snapping turtle

Snapping Turtle.
Painting by Margaret
Bakely of Vincentown.
Photograph by Dennis
McDonald.
PFP235202−1−25.

lunging at two ducks, is captured on canvas by Margaret Bakely, in a striking image of predation. Central to her painting are the turtle's giant jaws, a
much ruminated topic among local people, who all know that a snapper
can bite long after its head has been severed. The saying is that only two
things will cause it to release its grip: thunder or the setting sun.

Such beliefs about animals, usually attributed to old-timers, may seem
naive and misinformed to the scientific observer. Old-timers along the
Maurice River used to say that railbirds turn into frogs. Albert Reeves, an
old timer and well-known teller of landscapes there, gives them the benefit
of the doubt:

In ancient times, those old elves there, some of them thought that birds
turned into different things. . . . Well, a beautiful butterfly was nothing
but a worm, wasn't he at one time? Wasn't he? He was like a worm, and

when he comes out of that thing, and he's in there—you know in the cocoon—he turns into a beautiful butterfly, doesn't he? . . . So why can't a railbird turn into a frog?[61]

The fact is that, in the experience of mudwallopers, there is a mystifying relationship between frogs and railbirds, and snapping turtles (dead or alive) are unbelievably tenacious. People offering folk explanations for such phenomena often do not profess to believe them. Like natural phenomena, such explanations are themselves food for the imagination. They are literary resources in oral tradition that vivify life in the region.

Thus far we have considered a variety of ways in which the inner and outer landscapes mutually affect each other in literal and figurative realms; how it is that people cast form and meaning upon their surroundings, which in turn sustain them both physically and aesthetically. Many of the expressions we have looked at relate to ways in which people decipher, organize, and interpret the landscapes, turning them into backdrops for dramas in which animals are often the players.

On closer inspection of some of these rituals and stories about animals, we discover the outer landscape reflecting the inner landscape in complex ways. Through behaviors like bird feeding, turtle marking, and fox hunting, for example, people construct natural texts that simultaneously explore and reflect the social and natural orders. They get animals to tell them stories about themselves.[62]

The ubiquitous bird feeder, for example, is like a small theater, often viewed between the curtains of kitchen windows. Ethnobotanist Eugene Hunn compared one birdfeeder to a morality play, having witnessed through the eyes of its keeper, Leo Landy of Nesco, a cast of "spartan" chickadees, "proletarian" sparrows, "lazy" cardinals, "mild-mannered" doves, and "aggressive" bluejays who disdain anything but sunflower seeds. "That's the biggest robbers there are, blue jays," said Elwood Watson, of Wading River. Landy's feeder is sparingly stocked with sunflower seeds, to keep the jays from becoming like "welfare types."[63] This observation of the natural world gives rise to myriad stories through which the animal world continues to mirror the human one, as it has done for thousands of years.

Sense of place is one of the gifts that old people give. In Cumberland County, box turtles are made to represent the Brown family tree. Whenever a child has been born to Tom Brown, or a grandchild or a great-grandchild, Tom has inscribed the child's name and birthdate on the shell of a box turtle, according to a custom in Cumberland County:

Now I got a box turtle that's come back every year for twenty-seven years. Twenty-seven years ago I put "Pop-Pop" and "Dawn" on it, and put the date, and it come back again this year. It's blind. It's been blind for about five years, but it comes right to the back door and my wife'll feed it bread and we put it down in the window box for a few days and then release it. And this year, one I did for the great-granddaughter Muriel, I only just did that in '81, that one come back. [64]

Thus a living family register moves through varied landscapes on the shells of turtles.

Fox hunting is an elaborate ritual in which the quarry is more often protected than taken at the end. Any fox hunter will say that the whole purpose of chasing foxes is to hear music from the dogs. Hound dogs are for many local people what binoculars are for birders. The stories that hounds deliver are not only about the natural world, but about the hunters, for whom the hounds are extensions into the natural world, and for whom they substitute in the pack. "You stand there at night," said Milton Collins of Port Republic, "you don't see anything. That sound comes to you, and there's a beautiful *story* in it. I know that it's my dog just picked up the double and then Robly's dog took the double away from my dog, and he's runnin' it, or she's runnin' it." [65]

What *is* the story? Like other rituals, fox hunting mirrors its participants. According to fox hunters, a working dog is like a working man: it

Maryland hound dog. Drawing by Allen Carroll.

doesn't matter what he looks like, as long as he does his job. The elements of fox, dogs, landscape, and men are always the same. In each chase the themes of everyday life are recapitulated. Through their dogs the men aspire to a united effort—the production of a rich, orchestral sound. The dogs should "pack up" so tightly, as Norman Taylor said, that you could throw a blanket over them. However, there should not be so many of them that hunters cannot pick out the individual notes. The hunters also compete with one another through their dogs. They expect sportsmanlike behavior from their dogs, who should enact the social code that hard work, not laziness, will be rewarded. "I'd like to tell you a story that I just remembered," said John Earlin, of Browns Mills.

Many years ago, Ben was runnin' a fox on the east side of [Rt.] 539, and I was trailin' a fox on the west side, and after a bit, our dogs got together. At that time I had an old Black-and-Tan dog that I . . . hadn't ever seen 'im run before. And my dogs and Ben got in, and they were really doin' the job on this gray fox. They were takin' him around and around and around. And my old Black-and-Tan, he just stood there and listened. And they run 'im maybe for an hour, an hour and a half. And out he came and he came right in the middle of the road. He run right up there, and the Black-and-Tan stood right in the middle of the road, and the old fox went right between the legs of the Black-and-Tan, and he turned around and *caught* him. And I mean to tell you, you want to hear a man that really was mad, that was Ben. He said, "The worthless son-of-a-gun," he said. "Can you imagine a dog that wouldn't run nothin', catchin' that fox!" Now he was very unhappy about the whole situation, and I couldn't hardly blame him. I think that the dog should have showed some sign of going in there.[66]

At the juncture of nature and culture, hound dogs deliver information about the unseen landscape to the listening hunters. They also enact social conflicts: the collective versus the individual, music versus din, fair versus foul play, domestic order versus the wild unknown, and merit versus chance. A pack of hounds is like a book on a shelf, and each time the hunters open it up, a new story on the old themes emerges, telling the landscapes afresh.

NOTES

1. Barry Lopez, "Story at Anaktuvuk Pass: At the Juncture of Landscape and Narrative," *Harper's* (December 1984): 49–52.

2. Herbert Halpert, "Folktales and Legends from the New Jersey Pines: A Collection and a Study" (Ph.D. dissertation, Indiana University, 1947), I:18–19.

3. Excerpt from "The Pine Barrens Song," written by Merce Ridgway, Sr., New Gretna, NJ, 1978. Permission to quote granted by Merce Ridgway, Jr.

4. J. B. Jackson, "Landscapes as Theater," *Landscape* 23 (1979): 1.

5. Interview, Jens Lund with Louis Peterson, October 22, 1983, PFP83–RJL019, Pinelands Folklife Project Archive, American Folklife Center, Library of Congress. Hereafter, references to archive materials will be listed with names, date, and data retrieval number only.

6. Correspondence, Joanne Van Istendal to Mary Hufford, May 1984.

7. Interview, Mary Hufford with Herbert Payne, May 1979.

8. Interview, Mary Hufford with Harry Payne, November 14, 1983, PFP83–RMH031.

9. Gerald Parsons, "Suggestions Concerning the Study of Fur Trapping in the New Jersey Pinelands Project," United States Government Memorandum, Library of Congress, August 13, 1983.

10. Harold F. Wilson, *The Jersey Shore: A Social and Economic History of the Counties of Atlantic, Cape May, Monmouth and Ocean* (New York: Lewis Historical Publishing Company, Inc., 1953) II:724.

11. Interview, Eugene Hunn with Tom Brown, December 1983, PFP83–AEH008.

12. Elizabeth White, personal communication, 1953, cited in William Bolger, Herbert J. Githens, and Edward S. Rutsch, "Historic Architectural Survey and Preservation Planning Project for the Village of Whitesbog, Burlington and Ocean Counties, New Jersey (Morristown, NJ: New Jersey Conservation Foundation, September 1982), 46.

13. Aldo Leopold, "The Conservation Esthetic," in *A Sand County Almanac* (New York: Oxford University Press, 1949), 173.

14. Interview, Mary Hufford with members of Spartan Gun Club, November 17, 1983, PFP83–RMH044.

15. Interview, Mary Hufford with Larry Carpenter, November 19, 1983, PFP83–RMH046.

16. Interview, Eugene Hunn with Jim Stasz, December 19, 1983, PFP83–AEH006.

17. Fieldnotes, Eugene Hunn, December 18, 1983, PFP83–FEH1218.

18. Franz Boas, *Primitive Art* (Irvington-on-Hudson, NY: Capitol Publishing Company, Inc., 1951), 9.

19. Dell Hymes, "Folklore's Nature and the Sun's Myth," *Journal of American Folklore* 88 (1975): 348.

20. Kevin Lynch, *The Image of the City* (Cambridge: MIT Press, 1960), 127.

21. Kay Young, "Ethnobotany: A Methodology for Folklorists" (M.A. thesis, Western Kentucky University, 1983), 22.

22. For a discussion of the difference between "knowledge about" and "knowledge of," see Susanne Langer, *An Introduction to Symbolic Logic* (New York: Dover Publications, Inc., 1967), 22–23. Jonathan Berger and John Sinton emphasize the need to combine scientific and experiential perspectives (which they call "cognized" and "operational," respectively, after anthropologist Roy Rappoport) in the management of the Pinelands National Reserve in *Water, Earth and Fire: Land Use and Environmental Planning in the New Jersey Pine Barrens* (Baltimore: Johns Hopkins University Press, 1985), 203–206.

23. Interview, Eugene Hunn with Jack Cervetto, June 22, 1984, PFP84–AEH014.

24. Lynch, *Image,* 127.

25. Interview, Mary Hufford with Richard Gille, September 23, 1983, PFP83–AMH008.

26. Interview, Mary Hufford with Jack and Ann Davis, September 19, 1983, PFP83–RMH010.

27. Interview, Mary Hufford with Joe Albert, August 22, 1982.

28. Hufford with members of Spartan Gun Club, PFP83–RMH044.

29. Interview, Mary Hufford with Frank Day, September 19, 1983, PFP83–RMH016.

30. Interview, Nora Rubinstein with Jack Cervetto, October 28, 1983, PFP83–ANR003.

31. Interview, Mary Hufford with Clifford Frazee, September 23, 1983, PFP83–RMH012.

32. Interview, Mary Hufford with Norman Taylor and Caroline Taylor, September 22, 1983, PFP83–AMH006.

33. Interview, Mal O'Connor with Mary Lamonaca, June 20, 1985, PFP85–AMO001.

34. Interview, Mal O'Connor with Eddie Lamonaca, June 25, 1985, PFP85–AMO005.

35. Fieldnotes, Bonnie Blair, November 11, 1983, PFP83–FBB1111.

36. The concept of "great" and "little" traditions is drawn

from Robert Redfield's formulation in *The Little Community* (Chicago: University of Chicago Press, 1956).

37. Interview, Elaine Thatcher and Sue Samuelson with Clara Paolino, October 11, 1983, PFP83–RET016.

38. Interview, Mary Hufford with Ann Davis, September 19, 1983, PFP83–RMH009.

39. Paula Johnson, "Sloppy Work For Women: Oyster Shucking in Southern Maryland" (Paper presented at the American Folklore Society 1984 Annual Meeting, San Diego, California, October 11, 1984).

40. Interview, Rita Moonsammy with Beryl Whittington, November 1982, PFP83–ARM011.

41. Paul Shepard, *Man in the Landscape: A Historic View of the Esthetics of Nature* (New York: Alfred A. Knopf, 1967), 47.

42. O'Connor with Eddie Lamonaca, PFP85–AMO005.

43. Interview, Jens Lund with George Campbell, November 7, 1983, PFP83–RJL023.

44. Boas, *Primitive Art*, 10.

45. Lund with Peterson, PFP83–RJL017.

46. Interview, Tom Carroll and Nora Rubinstein with Ed Hazelton, November 4, 1983, PFP83–RTC005.

47. Interview, Jens Lund with Ted Von Bosse, September 21, 1983, PFP83–RJL003.

48. Interview, Tom Carroll and Nora Rubinstein with Ed Hazelton, November 4, 1983, PFP83–RNR011.

49. Ibid.

50. Interview, Christopher Hoare with Sam Hunt, April 28, 1978, quoted in David Steven Cohen, *The Folklore and Folklife of New Jersey* (New Brunswick, NJ: Rutgers University Press, 1983), 122.

51. Hufford with Davis, PFP83–RMH009.

52. Interview, Mary Hufford with Norman Taylor, November 1980.

53. Jackson, "Landscapes as Theater," 7.

54. John McPhee, *The Pine Barrens* (New York: Farrar, Strauss and Giroux, 1968), 9.

55. Fieldnotes, Mary Hufford, April 8, 1984, PFP84–FMH0408.

56. Hunn with Brown, PFP83–AEH008.

57. Hunn with Cervetto, PFP84–AEH014. Hunn speculates that this species is *Lampropeltis getulis getulis,* the eastern king snake, based on local descriptions and Roger Conant's allusion to it as "swamp wamper" in *A Field Guide to Reptiles and Amphibians of Eastern and Central America,* 2nd ed. (Boston: Houghton, 1975), 202.

58. Robert Plant Armstrong, *The Affecting Presence: An Essay in Humanistic Anthropology* (Urbana, IL: University of Illinois Press, 1971).

59. David Wilson, *In the Presence of Nature* (Amherst: University of Massachusetts Press, 1978), 1.

60. Interview, Rita Moonsammy with Tom Brown, February 17, 1982.

61. Interview, Gerald Parsons with Albert Reeves, September 24, 1984, PFP84–RGP006.

62. Clifford Geertz, "Deep Play: Notes on the Balinese Cockfight," in *The Interpretation of Cultures* (New York: Basic Books, 1973) 448.

63. Fieldnotes, Eugene Hunn, December 20, 1983, PFP83–FEH1220.

64. Interview, Mary Hufford with Tom Brown, June 1984.

65. Interview, Mary Hufford with Milton Collins, December 1980.

66. Tape of fox-hunting recollections, John Earlin, Browns Mills, New Jersey.

CREATING THE LANDSCAPE:

Historic Human Ecology of the Pinelands

N O LESS THAN IN ANY OTHER REGION, IN THE PINES THE history of settlement patterns and resource use is reflected in its various landscapes and in the contemporary activities of its residents. And, as in other regions, the array of relationships and activities is stunning. It includes the fishing, gunning, trapping, and recreational landscapes of the coastal areas, as well as the forests, bogs, fields, and military installations of the uplands.

The forces which created the human ecology and landscapes of the Pines stem from the geographic happenstance of the Pinelands' location between New York City and Philadelphia; from the indigenous cultures of the people who settled here; and from the great social, political, and economic forces, such as the Industrial Revolution, which changed the entire nation. The Pinelands is, therefore, the product of its own special circumstances as well as a reflection of regional and national trends. As J. B. Jackson wrote recently:

No group sets out to create a landscape, of course. What it sets out to do is to create a community, and the landscape as its visible manifestation is simply the by-product of people working and living, sometimes coming together, sometimes staying apart, but always recognizing their interdependence. . . . Like a language, a landscape will have obscure and inde-

John W. Sinton

Opposite: *Detail, Apple harvest, Cumberland County. Courtesy of the Donald A. Sinclair New Jersey Collection. Special Collections and Archives, Rutgers University Libraries.*

43

cipherable origins, like a language it is the slow creation of all elements in society. It grows according to its own laws, rejecting or accepting neologisms as it sees fit, clinging to obsolescent forms, inventing new ones. A landscape, like a language, is the field of perpetual conflict and compromise between what is established by authority and what the vernacular insists upon preferring.[1]

The history of human ecology in the Pinelands can be divided into three periods based on major changes in the social and economic structures of the northeastern United States and the nation as a whole. The first period spans the seventeenth, eighteenth, and nineteenth centuries. Dutch, English, and New England settlers, followed by northern Europeans and blacks, came down the coast and up the rivers to harvest woods, water, and farmlands. During the second period, beginning in the 1850s, railroads brought immigrant groups from Germany, Italy, and Eastern Europe into the Pinelands. At what must have seemed like isolated spots, they established towns like those they had left: Egg Harbor City, Vineland, and Woodbine. The railroads aided the growth of truck farming, fruit farming, and tourism by linking the region with the cities. Speculators sold quarter-acre lots on what were no more than paper streets. After World War II, the third period brought suburban and second-home developments to the Pinelands.[2]

Depending on the technology of the period and the economic demand for various resources, whether fish, wood, or potable water, different sections of the Pinelands were used for different purposes. In the first half of the first historic period, from about 1680, settlement took place principally along the coasts and navigable rivers. The primary activities were maritime industries, especially shipbuilding, and subsistence agriculture. Between 1760 (the founding of the first ironworks) and 1860, the rural industries of iron manufacturing and glassmaking thrived and died. During the second period, from 1860 until 1950, berry agriculture replaced rural industry in the forest regions, while small manufacturing, commercial agriculture, and recreation increased commensurately. After World War II, residential developments grew rapidly along the coast, while small manufacturing and agriculture declined in the interior.

The first period, from 1680 to 1860, encompassed the first coastal settlements, the beginning of the Civil War, and the arrival of the railroads, and coincided with the high tide of the Industrial Revolution. This period set the broad patterns of landscapes, resource use, settlement, and cultural life that still exist in the Pinelands National Reserve—the basic elements that contribute to the contemporary sense of place.

Two overriding geographic factors laid the foundations of the human ecology that has developed over the past 300 years. First was the simple fact that the Pinelands is located near two of America's largest cities—Philadelphia and New York. The Pinelands, therefore, participated in the birth of the nation and had direct connections to the cultural and political life of what would become a megalopolis. Second, the sandy composition of most Pinelands soil limited its attractiveness to early agricultural settlers. This fact, coupled with the lack of a physical site for a major city along the coast or the Delaware estuary, dictated that the Pinelands would become what Jane Jacobs calls a "supply region," destined to supply materials, people, and services to Philadelphia and New York rather than to become a major economic generator itself. In short, the Pinelands was to remain an appendage, a situation which brought both benefits and curses. While the region could retain its rural character, it would never be able to generate enough economic activity to enrich all its residents. While Pinelands people would have the use of the region's water, woods, and wildlife, much of the land would be owned by more wealthy outsiders. While those who chose to remain in the Pines could live within the seasonal rhythms of the place, they would lose many of the young people to the excitement and riches of the cities. And, during the most recent historic period, a long series of struggles would develop between those who wanted to retain the rural character of the Pines and those who wanted to convert much of the region into metropolitan bedroom communities.

On top of the geographic factors were laid the economic activities and settlement patterns as determined by eighteenth- and nineteenth-century technology and the social and cultural composition of the settlers. The human ecology of that early period can best be appreciated by looking at a map of the Tuckahoe area, which was typical of most other parts of the Pines at that time. Tuckahoe is in the southeast section of the Pinelands region, 15 air miles from Atlantic City. The most outstanding features on the map are the nine sawmills in a 50-square mile area, all built between 1737 and 1812. The original sawmills and ponds, around which small communities of three or four households gathered, served the larger coastal and estuarine villages with their shipbuilding and commercial activities. An 1834 gazeteer described Tuckahoe as follows:

Tuckahoe, port town on both sides of the Tuckahoe river, over which there is a bridge, ten miles above the sea, forty-six miles southeast from Woodbury (the county seat), and by post-route 192 from Washington, D.C.: contains some twenty buildings, three taverns, several stores. It is

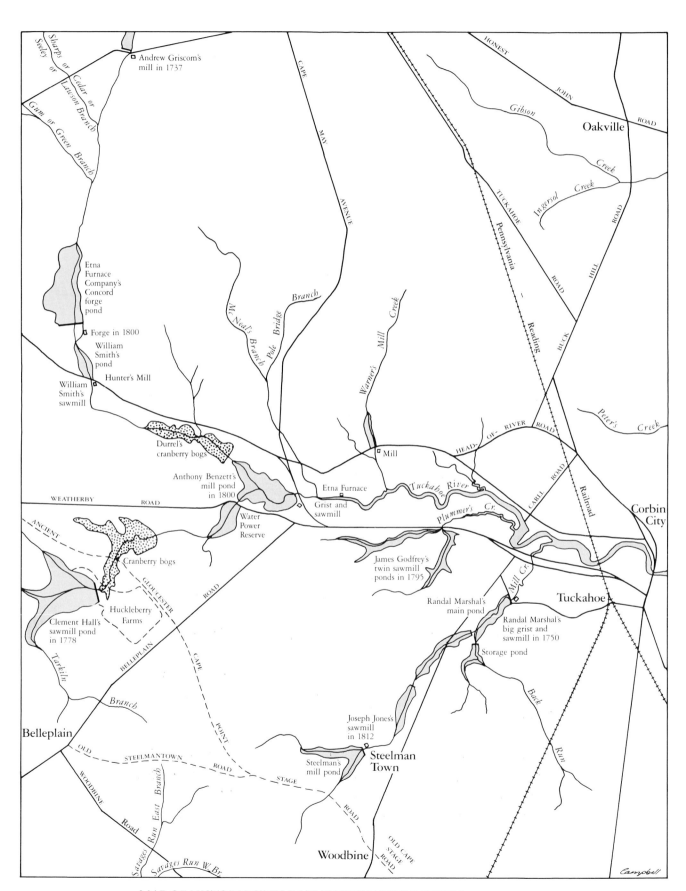

MAP OF HISTORIC SITES IN THE TUCKAHOE REGION
BASED ON A FIELD SURVEY BY CHARLES HARTMAN OF MILLVILLE
(1979)

a place of considerable trade in wood, lumber, and ship building. The land immediately on the river is good, but a short distance from it, is swampy and low.[3]

All the resource-based activities which occurred in the coastal and southern uplands region also took place in the Tuckahoe area, from fishing and shipbuilding to farming, logging, and iron making. The most important long-term activities centered on the coast. Tuckahoe was just one of many small Jersey coastal towns producing boats during the eighteenth, nineteenth, and early twentieth centuries.[4] The shipyards were the hub of economic life in the Pines for 200 years, and almost all of them were on navigable rivers, far enough upstream to be protected from northeast storms and hurricanes. Like other shipyards, the one in Tuckahoe probably produced its share of schooners over 100 tons, although most were in the 30- to 60-ton range.

In 1900 New Jersey had the largest working sailing fleet in the country, and most of the vessels were produced in South Jersey. With its demand for men and materials, this huge industry supported a wide range of auxiliary enterprises. Many kinds of wood and wood products (such as tar), as well as textiles, iron, glass, tallow, sulfur, and paint, were used in boats. The skills of carpenters, shipwrights, sawyers, joiners, carvers, caulkers, sealers, instrument makers, glaziers, blacksmiths, upholsterers, and chairmakers were required. Because the market for boats fluctuates, however, many workers had to combine several skills rather than depend solely on boatbuilding for a living.[5]

While boat- and shipbuilding provided coastal residents with most of their cash, their lives were also patterned around seasonal activities to harvest the rich resources of the environment: fishing and shellfishing, gunning, trapping, salt haying, farming, and logging. These are all activities which have continued to the present day.

It is important to understand both the richness of the coastal resources and, as can be seen from the Tuckahoe map, the relationship between the coastal areas and the forest regions, because it was the rural industries of the forest which fed the larger, more permanent communities along the coast.

The map of the Tuckahoe region shows numerous small mills scattered along all the watercourses. The earliest date for a sawmill or gristmill is 1737, for the Andrew Griscom mill in the northwest corner of the map, well inland from a coastal center and quite near Mays Landing. This location suggests that the inland sections of the Pinelands were settled before

F. L. MULFORD, PR

the advent of the iron furnace towns. By extrapolation we can assume that a significant amount of activity was taking place throughout the forest regions of the Pines during the eighteenth century. We can also assume that by the middle of the nineteenth century, almost every river and stream in the Pines had been dammed for some use, whether for iron or glass, or, more commonly, lumber and grist milling. All these mill communities

YARD

ILLVILLE, CUMBERLAND CO. N.J

were tied directly to the larger, more permanent coastal communities by waterways or sand roads.

    We have no real documentation about these early communities other than notations in deeds and probates or archeological evidence. We do not really know what sort of people settled these hamlets, but their names suggest English or New England origins. The technologies they used for mill-

Mulford's Shipyard on the Maurice River at Millville, 1875. From Atlas of Cumberland County. *Philadelphia: D. J. Stewart, 1876.*

Sawmill at New Lisbon, 1894. Photograph by Nathaniel R. Ewan. Courtesy of the Burlington County Historical Society.

ing and lumbering and the kind of houses they built were similar to those found throughout the northeast United States at the time. The products they produced and the ships they built in the coastal towns were commercially valuable to merchants not only in Philadelphia and, later, New York, but to the English, who had denuded their own forests for wartime shipbuilding in the seventeenth century and were in dire need of timber from the American colonies.

From their earliest settlement, then, Pinelands communities were connected to a larger region—indeed, to world commerce. The patterns of Pinelands towns, even the architecture of the houses, were derived from general patterns found in England and the Northeast, and the dominant religion, Quakerism, stemmed from the same cultural background. Some old coastal towns, such as Barnegat and Tuckerton, still preserve part of their original character, and many of the eighteenth-century houses stand today, testaments to the original settlers.[6]

By 1760, when the first Pinelands iron furnace was founded at Batsto, the social and geographic patterns of the first historic period were already established. The creation of the so-called iron "plantations" in the Pines (approximately two dozen in all between 1760 and 1850) was triggered by growth in both the population and the self-sufficiency of the Colonies as they broke away from England. The Pinelands was a particularly appropriate place in which to found iron manufacturing because of its proximity to Philadelphia with her ready markets and capital, and its richness in the resources that were necessary for iron making, especially wood for fuel.

The period from 1810 to 1860 was a busy industrial time not only for the forest regions of the Pinelands, but also for the rural Northeast as a whole. The Industrial Revolution was just beginning, but meanwhile most industrial products were being produced in rural areas which used wood for fuel and water for power. In addition to the two dozen iron furnaces in the Pines, there appeared a smaller number of forges and slitting mills. Beginning about 1800, a series of 20 glass factories were founded. Most had died by 1870. Some lasted to 1930, and a few were transformed into the modern glass industry around Millville. There were also several paper mills, which used salt hay (*Spartina*) for raw material, and cotton factories, which produced cloth from rags.

The principal natural resource on which rural industry rested was wood, and because of this, people continually cut the woodlands, from the smallest pitch pine to the largest cedar. The enormous demand for wood,

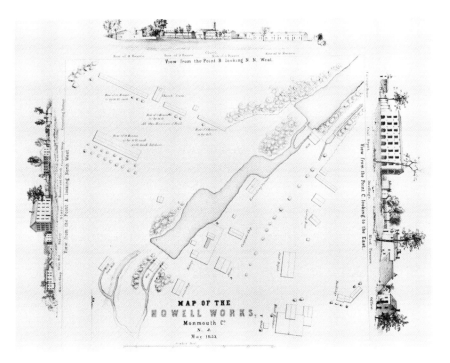

Map of the Howell Iron Works, Monmouth County, 1853. Courtesy of the Monmouth County Historical Association.

coupled with uncontrollable forest fires, drastically changed the landscape of the region from its earlier form.

A medium-sized iron furnace, such as the one at Batsto that produced some 900 tons of iron annually, required about 6,000 cords of wood per year for the 12,000 bushels of charcoal used to fire its furnaces. Forests in the Pinelands generally produce only one-third to one-half a cord of wood per acre per year. A conservative estimate is that the five furnaces in the Batsto area (the Wharton Tract) would have required 40,000 acres of woodland annually for their production. But in fact more wood was needed because in that same area were three forges, four glasshouses, a paper mill, and a cotton mill. Furthermore, oak had to be cut for domestic fuel and cedar for

Winslow Glass Works, Camden County. Courtesy of the Donald A. Sinclair New Jersey Collection. Special Collections and Archives, Rutgers University Libraries.

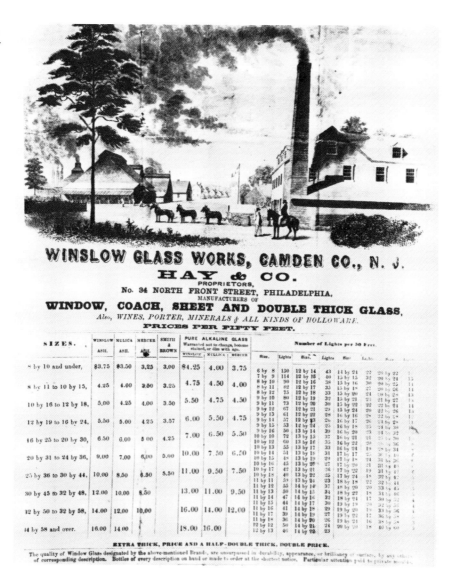

boatbuilding and shingle production. Coppice, or young oak growth, was cut for hoop-poles, for barrels, for pole wood, and for basketmaking. Most economic activities in the Pines depended on wood and hardly a man was born in the forest regions who, at one time or another, did not cut wood or fell trees.[7]

The Atlantic white cedar of the wetlands was and still is by far the most valuable tree in the Pines, as much because of its scarcity as because of its irreplaceable qualities of light weight and resistance to weather and disease. It is in high demand for roofing, fence posts, and boats. Oak is most valuable as a mature tree for construction and in small pieces for heating fuel. Pitch pine was, during the first historic period, the most useful wood because it was essential to industry. Small trees were cut mostly for charcoal, but some large pines were used for construction, poles, and later for railroad ties and newspaper pulp.

The insatiable demand for wood from the Pines throughout the nineteenth century required that the whole region be cut several times over. Each year the woodcutters and colliers combed their areas for new sources of wood and cut everything one inch in diameter and up. They then moved to the next woodlot, leaving slash and sand behind them, and sometimes even

George C. Rowand charcoal burner's cabin, MacDonald's Branch, Lebanon State Forest, 1927. Courtesy of George H. Pierson, New Jersey Bureau of Forest Management, Division of Parks and Forestry.

purposely burned the site so they could purchase it cheaply and harvest it 15 years later. Further, wildfires claimed tens of thousands of acres of forest every decade. Reports from the *New Jersey State Geologist* in the late nineteenth century are filled with descriptions of fires that burned 10, 20, or 30 thousand acres at a time. A hundred years ago much of the Pinelands looked barren indeed—a forest devastated by axmen and wildfires.[8]

Did nineteenth-century people understand that they were destroying their forests? Perhaps we need to understand what destruction and creation meant to them and to explore what was economically important to those people rather than aesthetically important to us. At what point in the life of a forest—in terms of ecological succession—could the rural industrialists expect to get the species of trees they needed to support their economy? Put most simply, how could people in the nineteenth century get the most cedar and pine in the shortest time possible?

Had the people of the Pines been ardent conservationists a hundred years ago and protected their forests from fire and cutting, they would have produced precisely the kind of woodland least useful to their economy, since climax conditions result in oak and mixed swamp-hardwood stands. People needed pine and cedar, which generally occur early in succession and, in fact, cannot regenerate extensive stands unless they are disturbed. By cutting forests and starting fires intentionally, the people of the Pines were, in ecological terms, keeping the forest in an early successional stage and, in economic terms, assuring themselves of the kinds of wood, especially pine, necessary to support their industries.

In 1860, after three generations of heavy cutting and burning, the Pines were certainly barren. Photographs from the turn of the century show desolate backgrounds, barren land, and slash piles. But the regenerative powers of even this poor soil were suufficient to supply nineteenth-century industrial needs. Out of the ashes and stumps and roots grew the pines that made the wood and charcoal that ran the furnaces, forges, and glasshouses. Every 20 years the wood choppers and colliers gathered their harvest on a given site, and the cycle of the phoenix continued until the industries died.[9]

Industrialization of the forest regions also meant drastic changes in settlement patterns, and for a hundred years the forest provided habitation for at least twice the number of people now living there. Following is a contemporary description of a typical iron town, this one in Weymouth near Mays Landing:

Weymouth, blast furnace, forge and village, in Hamilton Township, Gloucester County, upon the Great Egg Harbour River, about five miles

above the head of navigation. The furnace makes about 900 tons of casting annually: the forge having four fires and two hammers, makes about 200 tons bar iron, immediately from the ore. There are also a grist and a saw mill, and buildings for the workmen, of whom 100 are constantly employed about the works, and the persons depending upon them for subsistence, average 600 annually. There are 85,000 acres of land pertaining to this establishment. . . . The works have a superabundant supply of water, during all seasons of the year.[10]

Aerial view of Batsto. Courtesy of the Office of New Jersey Heritage, Division of Parks and Forestry.

All the connotations of the word "plantation" were appropriate for the iron towns which the Philadelphia Quakers established. The most important plantation owners were the Richardses of Philadelphia, who created, in Arthur Pierce's words, an "Empire in the Pines." The family bought huge tracts of forest land, the borders of which were contiguous, so that a pattern of large-sized land holdings was established. The result was to create outside ownership of much of the forest region, some of which still exists today in the hands of speculators and developers. Other large forest tracts are held by local residents who are cranberry farmers.

The central place in these tracts was the iron village, and in the center of the iron village was the owner's mansion.

Batsto was the seat of the Richards's paternalistic empire, and their rambling, wooden mansion was the center of authority and social life in the village. In addition to the family, the mansion housed servants and unmarried workers, who lived in basement quarters. Near the mansion were a gristmill, sawmill, spring house, summer house, garden and orchard, smokehouses, and barns. Across the millpond were workers' cottages, gardens, and outbuildings. The workers, who came from Europe, other forges, and employees' families, enjoyed secure, well paid jobs and active social lives. Long tenure of skilled workers was common.[11]

The residents of the rural industrial towns were individuals from families who had settled there in the eighteenth century as well as immigrants from northern Europe and a few blacks whom the Quakers had helped to come north on the Underground Railway. While there were a few Catholics in the Pines, chiefly Irish immigrants, most of the residents had become Methodists by the first quarter of the nineteenth century. The Methodist circuit riders of the early 1800s had achieved a clear success in the Pinelands against the rival Episcopalians and Presbyterians. To this day, Methodism exerts a strong influence in Pinelands towns, and the church continues to play the principal role in the social life of women there.

By mid-century the tide of the Industrial Revolution caught up with the rural industries, not only in the Pinelands, but throughout the Northeast. New technologies in industry and transportation emptied all the rural industrial areas of the region as well as those of New York and New England. Within a generation, the population of the Pinelands was cut in half as workers and their families moved to the cities. The pine woods, sand, and bog iron were no longer useful to an industrializing society.

When revolutionary technological, economic, and social changes occur, however, some of the old ways of life are always left to mix with the new. Some activities from the first historic period continued into the second, which spanned the years from 1860 to 1950: fishing, gunning, trapping, salt haying, and to a lesser extent, boatbuilding. Some activities increased, such as agriculture, and some new activities appeared: plant gathering and collecting, cranberrying and commercial blueberrying, working on military installations, small manufacturing (mostly of clothing), and catering to tourism.

The impetus for economic growth came chiefly from railroads, which opened access to urban markets for goods and services from the Pinelands region. The most lasting impact was to cut the Pines into two sections, north and south of the Mullica River. Because the two major east-west lines ran to the tourist resorts of Atlantic City and Cape May, a rail net developed

throughout the southern section, while the northern section had no east-west link, only one that ran north-south through the central, least populated, areas.

The rail net south of the Mullica spawned truck farms and orchards, health spas and boondoggle real-estate developments, small clothing industries, and ethnic settlements. Although large tracts of forest remained for charcoal makers and loggers to work, much of it was turned into fields—the higher ground for peaches, apples, tomatoes, cucumbers, and sweet and white potatoes, and the wetter ground for blueberries, which were cultivated after World War I by Elizabeth White at Whitesbog near Browns Mills. In addition, cranberry fever hit the region in the 1860s, and landowners and lessees turned old millponds and swamps into cranberry bogs. An enormous amount of cedar was lost as the trees were drowned and cut to make way for new bogs. The map of the Tuckahoe region illustrates these patterns from the second historic period with its cranberry bogs, blueberry fields, and rail lines.

As it did throughout America, the railroad also created new speculative

Apple harvest, Cumberland County. Courtesy of the Donald A. Sinclair New Jersey Collection. Special Collections and Archives, Rutgers University Libraries.

and settlement opportunities in the Pinelands. Italians, Germans, and Eastern European Jews settled in ethnic communities in the southern region. Some came as railroad workers, while others bought or were given land by German Protestant and Jewish philanthropists. The Jews of Woodbine, the Germans of Egg Harbor City, and the Italians of Hammonton built self-contained agricultural and industrial communities and thrived; their economic preeminence held until after World War II. Speculators, including railway companies, bought cheap forest land and advertised

Jewish farm family, Woodbine, circa 1900. From William Stainsby, The Jewish Colonies of South Jersey. *Camden: Chew and Sons, 1901.*

small lots to anyone foolish enough to buy them. Speculative development littered the maps of the southern Pinelands, almost all of them failures like Montefiore, Gigantic City, and Little Italy. In the late nineteenth century, New York and Philadelphia newspapers commonly gave away small pieces of ground in the Pinelands with new subscriptions.

North of the Mullica River, speculators and cranberry operators also flourished. As happened in the southern Pines, few developments succeeded. Paisley and Fruitland, for example, are now mere curiosities. Because the watersheds were somewhat larger there than in the south, and competing land uses fewer, extensive cranberry bogs still exist. The old rural industrial towns and outlying villages, however, are now lost in the woods. No railroads came to reinvigorate the economy, so the northern Pinelands slowly returned to woods, swamps, and bogs after the Civil War. Woodcutters, colliers, gatherers, hunters, and berry cultivators exploited the section of the Pines no one else wanted.[12] These same patterns set the stage for most of what a traveler can see today on Pinelands landscapes.

And what happened to the people of the Pines during this period? As the saying goes: "You can always make a buck from the bay or a dollar in the woods." Those families who elected to remain lived with the rhythm of the seasons and followed the complex patterns of resource exploitation established by their predecessors. As the processes of industrialization and urbanization sped forward, the gap between rural and urban cultures widened to the point where metropolites looked on rural people as odd and backward. It was during this period that the stereotype of the "Piney" was born: the stories of strange and isolated people deep in the Pine woods, all of whom would shoot strangers on sight.

The root of the stereotype lies in the study of the Kallikak family that was conducted at the Vineland Training School in the first decade of this century by H. H. Goddard and his research assistant, Elizabeth Kite. Stephen Jay Gould studied Goddard's work and found that:

Goddard discovered a stock of paupers and ne'er-do-wells in the Pine Barrens of New Jersey and traced their ancestry back to the illicit union of an upstanding man with a supposedly feeble-minded tavern wench. The same man later married a worthy Quakeress and started another line composed wholly of upstanding citizens. Since the progenitor had fathered both a good and bad line, Goddard combined the Greek words for beauty (*kallos*) and bad (*kakos*), and awarded him the pseudonym Martin Kallikak.[13]

In fact, the family on which the Kallikak study was based was from Hunterdon County, not the Pines, as noted in a recent book by J. David Smith.[14]

In an absurd attempt to support the budding eugenics movement, Goddard and Kite traced the *kakos* family history through nine generations of alcoholism, blindness, criminality, deafness, epilepsy, insanity, syphilis, sexual immorality, tuberculosis, and feeblemindedness. The Goddard study was a hoax. Goddard's photographs, which he used as supporting evidence, "were phonied by inserting heavy dark lines to give eyes and mouths their diabolical appearance."[15] Even the tongues hanging out of the depraved mouths had been forged. Still, the stigma of the *kakos* line attached itself to all residents of the Pine Barrens.[16]

In fact, the rural people of the Pines lived not much differently from people in rural Pennsylvania, New York, or New England. They led independent lives in small communities centered on the Methodist church, and, in the early twentieth century, on gun clubs and volunteer fire companies. In the north, the pattern of large-scale land holdings continued. The Richards family was replaced with cranberry owners and another Quaker from Philadelphia, Joseph Wharton, who bought more than a hundred thousand acres of land in hopes that he could use the Mullica River basin as a source of potable water for Philadelphia.[17] When the state of New Jersey made out-of-state water shipments illegal, Wharton simply held the land in single ownership, and his heirs sold it in 1950 to the state, which established Wharton State Forest.

In other forest sections, speculators bought hundreds of thousands of acres in both large and small parcels, regardless of whether their titles were clear. Land speculation and confusing small landholdings are now part of the contemporary heritage of the Pines.

Still other parts of the Pinelands became cultural refuges for groups fleeing Europe. A great brick synagogue bears witness to the Jewish settlement in Woodbine during the 1890s, although few Jews are left, most of them having gone to nearby urban areas. Egg Harbor City was established by German immigrants in the 1850s, and the pattern of the town and its architecture reflect typical German burgher attitudes. Hammonton became a predominantly Italian town settled by emigrants from several communities in the Neapolitan region and Sicily during the 1860s and 1870s. Cassville in the northern Pines was settled after the Russian Revolution by Russian Orthodox groups and still serves as a major regional religious center. So long as land was cheap and immigrants plentiful, the Pinelands served them as a refuge, and the refugees added a great deal of cultural diversity to a region which, up until the mid-nineteenth century, had been culturally homogeneous.

Lastly, the railroad brought significant growth to coastal sections of the Pines. Atlantic City burgeoned in the 1870s as the playground for blue-collar workers from Philadelphia. Along the coast of northern Ocean County, recreational activities and summer home development grew slowly, so that many coastal residents were able to earn cash in the building trades as well as in older seasonal activities. The slow pace of change, however, would be threatened by new technological and social developments after World War II.

In the period following the war, from 1950 to 1985, two major shifts occurred: the small industrial complexes of the southern section began to die as industry continued to concentrate in metropolitan areas, and suburban, second-home, and retirement developments began to grow with the advent of the population boom and high-speed roads and automobiles.

The northern fringes of the Pinelands have borne the brunt of suburbanization since 1950, not so much because land was cheaper, but because the area was closer to Philadelphia and New York. Ocean County was the fastest-growing county in the United States between 1960 and 1980. Although the north-central section, the so-called "core" of the region, still displays some landscapes left from rural industrial and railroad periods, suburbs and retirement communities have nibbled off the borders all along the coastal and Delaware Valley sections. At times suburbs have leap-frogged over existing developments into the heartland, as has the retirement community of Leisure Village.

The southern section of the Pines, being farther from any metropolis, witnessed little suburbanization until recently and has seen its small industrial base die. Woodbine lost all its industries, and Egg Harbor is but a shadow of its old self; only Hammonton retains a solid but diminished industrial base. Along the coastal strip are miles of vacation homes, but few such developments have appeared inland, although significant tracts are now being set aside for camping. The southern section still bears the imprint of the second wave of settlement from the railroad, but, because of its proximity to Atlantic City casinos, it is finally under the pressure of suburbanization.

It is, nonetheless, surprising how similar a twentieth-century land use map is to one of the nineteenth-century. Today, residents of the Pinelands still use almost all the resources of the region that were used in the eighteenth and nineteenth centuries, from the shellfish of the bays to the wood of the forests to the water underground, and ties to land and resources are still important.

What is so valuable about the old ways, seasonal activities, and family and community ties? Though intrinsic interest in the old way of doing things is part of the value, the mutually advantageous balances between people and environment that are maintained in seasonal lifestyles are the greater value. The balances have evolved over time and have mediated changes in resources and demand. They have supported subsistence lifestyles independent of highly technological processes. But they are also based on interdependencies that suburbanization and industrialization tend to break apart. Once this happens, a whole series of adaptations also fall apart.[18]

What threatens the people of the Pines now is not change itself, but change that does not allow time for people's institutions and sense of place to settle into new patterns, and that, furthermore, may destroy crucial resources, whether clams or cedar. The attitudes of Pinelands residents do not differ significantly from those of residents of other areas. Some search for money, others for excitement and material goods, while most, like us, would like a whole mix of values even if the mix is unobtainable. The ways in which the people of the Pines work out their value systems and deal with their resources will decide the future of the region's landscapes and human ecology.

NOTES

1. John B. Jackson, *Discovering the Vernacular Landscape* (New Haven: Yale University Press, 1984), 12, 148.

2. Jonathan Berger and John W. Sinton, *Water, Earth, and Fire: Land Use and Environmental Planning in the New Jersey Pine Barrens* (Baltimore: Johns Hopkins University Press, 1985), 6.

3. Thomas Gordon, *A Gazetteer of the State of New Jersey* (Trenton: D. Fenton, 1834), 254.

4. Glenn S. Gordinier, "Maritime Enterprise in New Jersey: Great Egg Harbor During the Nineteenth Century," *New Jersey History* 97 (1979): 105–117.

5. Berger and Sinton, *Water, Earth, and Fire*, 62–63.

6. For more information on the South Jersey house, see Elizabeth Marsh, "The South Jersey House," in *History, Culture, and Archeology of the Pine Barrens*, ed. John W. Sinton (Pomona, NJ: Stockton State College, 1982), 185–187.

7. Berger and Sinton, *Water, Earth, and Fire*, 116.

8. Ibid., 117.

9. Ibid., 118.

10. Gordon, *Gazetteer*, 263.

11. Berger and Sinton, *Water, Earth, and Fire*, 64.

12. Ibid., 8–9.

13. Stephen Jay Gould, *The Mismeasure of Man* (New York: W. W. Norton, 1981), 168.

14. J. David Smith, *Minds Made Feeble: The Myth and Legacy of the Kallikaks* (Rockville, MD: Aspen, 1985).

15. Gould, *The Mismeasure of Man*, 168.

16. Berger and Sinton, *Water, Earth, and Fire*, 11.

17. Ibid., 66–67.

18. Ibid., 41.

LIVING WITH THE LANDSCAPE:

Folklife in the Environmental Subregions of the Pinelands

THROUGHOUT THE HISTORICAL PERIODS OF LAND USE IN the Pinelands, the traditional knowledge of place has enabled natives to shape the environment and harvest its resources, as well as to adapt to change. An important component of that knowledge has been the character of each of five major environmental subregions in the Pines: the pine and oak forests, the cedar and hardwood swamps, the meadows (salt- and fresh-water marshes), the rivers and bays, and the farmlands. Each of the first four has a special relationship to the underlying Cohansey Aquifer, and supports a characteristic array of flora and fauna. The farmlands are distinguished chiefly by their soils and type of use.

In the woodlands, where the water table is two feet or more beneath the sandy soil, pine and oak trees compete for light, water, and nutrients. In pine-oak forests, pines are more abundant than oak trees, and smaller scrub oaks and shrubs of black huckleberry and lowbush blueberry crowd beneath them. In oak-pine forests, on the other hand, leafy canopies of 50-foot oaks throw deep shadows over pine trees and shrubs. A wide variety of birds, as well as rabbit, fox, raccoon, squirrel, and deer, dwell in these forests. In the Pine Plains near Warren Grove, pygmy pines of less than six feet huddle with scrub oaks and mountain laurel. These dwarves, which hold their seed tightly in closed (serotinous) cones that only open in forest-'fire temperatures, have survived frequent fire through their ability to sprout from the stump after their crowns are burnt.

Opposite: *Detail. Cranberries being scooped, Hog Wallow, circa 1940. Photograph by William Augustine. Courtesy of the Donald A. Sinclair New Jersey Collection. Special Collections and Archives, Rutgers University Libraries.*

Rita Moonsammy / David S. Cohen / Mary T. Hufford

65

Interspersed throughout the forests and ribboned along rivers and streams are the swamps, the second type of environment. In a cedar swamp, the land dips near the aquifer, often along a stream bed, and acid soil and water nourish the tall, straight Atlantic white cedar. The water and soil are carpeted with spongy mats of sphagnum moss, and decorated with insectivorous plants such as sundews. In swamps where cedar has been cut off, hardwoods such as red maple and black gum now flourish.

In the meadowlands that skirt the woods and edge the rivers and bays, the water table reaches the surface. Plants such as broomsedge and bullsedge form tussocks in the flat, treeless freshwater marshes locally known as savannas. On the salt water meadows lining the coast, *Spartina* grasses are the dominant lifeform, with *Phragmites* (common reed), sedges, and rushes also growing along the brackish upper margins. Muskrat, mink, otter, beaver, and weasels inhabit the meadows, and waterfowl and shorebirds visit on their journeys up and down the Atlantic flyway.

The rivers that drain the Pinelands, and the bays of the Atlantic Ocean, into which they empty, are the fourth type of environment. They serve as transit routes for humans and as homes for many kinds of fish and shellfish. In the lower portions of rivers such as the Maurice and the Toms, marine fish such as the American shad and the striped bass spawn, while clams, crabs, and oysters populate the bays.

These four are the environments that nature created in the Pinelands. Humans created the fifth, the farmlands that have, over the years, been carved out of woodlands, swamps, and meadows. Their soils range from gravelly sand to sandy loam. In sandy, acid soils such as those classified as the Lakewood series, berries grow well. In those with more clay, such as the Sassafras series, vegetable farms prosper. Over time, people have learned to match soils and crops.

The folklife expressions that have been shaped by these environments, and that in turn have shaped them, are many. They range from the tools and processes that have been used to work the land, to the stories and pictures that reflect it. In all of these, as well as in the words of its natives, we may read the story of the Pinelands.

PINE AND OAK FORESTS

Lumbering

"Sawmills" wrote archeologist R. Alan Mounier, "are among the earliest and most durable sites of historic settlement in the Pine Barrens of New

Jersey."[1] Local wisdom underscores this scholarly observation in the saying "All the crossways lead to Candlewood." Located in Barnegat Township, Candlewood was one of the earliest sawmills. The remaining network of crossways (wooden roads) that surrounds it attests to the importance of sawmills in the early settlement of the woodlands. Many of these mills were built in the early eighteenth century to provide lumber for local ship- and house-building, as well as for export. Although they were scattered in isolated locations throughout the Pines, sawmill sites became centers for rural settlements and were followed over time by commercial activities such as gristmills, iron plantations, and cranberry bogs. Today the Pines is crisscrossed with roadways and dotted with place names and ruins that reflect that past: Braddock's Mill, Browns Mills, Pleasant Mills, Jones' Mill.

The two most important types of wood harvested in the uplands have been oak, used for ship- and home-building and basketmaking in the past, and for firewood in the present, and pine, used as fuel for Pinelands industries in the form of charcoal and cordwood. In the swamps that line stream beds in the woodlands grows the white cedar that has also been an important wood in the lumbering industry.

Because early sawmills were water powered, they had to be located near a water supply that could be dammed to make a "head of water," or millpond, from which a sluiceway would convey the water to the waterwheel. Because the streams of the Pinelands are generally shallow and slow moving, the waterwheels were probably "undershot," meaning that the water passed below, rather than above, the wheel. In about 1825, the circular saw replaced the vertical frame saw, and steam power replaced water in the latter part of the century. Early in the twentieth century, the internal combustion engine was introduced.

Today, the logging of numerous species of trees is usually done in small operations that include a wide range of technology. Jack Cervetto describes the engine that used to power his mill:

> That's a straight A Studebaker. '36. And that'd purr like a kitten when I was runnin' the mill. Run a belt from the driveshaft to the main pulley and that would run everything here. I had four or five saws there. And I got a well dug right alongside the motor, and then with a hose into the motor and the water would go in and come out the other side and keep the motor cool.[2]

George Brewer, Jr., of Dennisville eschews a highly automated setup and compares his mill with that of his father, George Sr., in an earlier time. "Our sawmill is very elementary. It's about as simple as you can get." It is

Interior of sawmill of Leroy Creamer of Dennisville. Photograph by Jens Lund. PFP216898-5-3.

diesel powered, and everything is cut on a head saw, because "with too much investment, you'd have to run a lot more material through to make it pay, and there's not that much available."[3]

Thorough knowledge of both the forest and the trees enables the woodsman to maintain himself. He can "read" in a stand of trees both its history and the kind of "bottom," or soil, that supports it. "If you find a bunch of pine in oak bottom, man has been there," explains Cervetto.[4] Early settlers once cleared oak stands to use the rich, loamy soil. Left untilled, however, the soil was quickly taken over by pines.

Fire, as well as humans, has also cleared land, and knowledge of its history can pay off:

See, there's a place back there. Now a forest fire hasn't been in there and see, those oaks are pretty good size. But this was all burned out in 1936. Clean killed all that. I cut that dead wood off for firewood. And that growed since 1936. There's nothing there to cut anything out of.[5]

Bottoms can affect safety and business as well as vegetation. "Sugar sand bottom" has caused travelers problems for years.

There's three hills below my house going to Tuckerton and two of 'em is sugar sand. So an automobile or even in horse and wagon days, they'd never go to Tuckerton on account of that. They'd cut right down in that sugar sand, of sand bottom. And you'll find pieces of it in different old roads through the woods. It's bad as clay bottom. It dries like concrete. Gets wet and it's like mud. Go right down to the axle.[6]

A woodsman must know the characteristics of different woods and their uses. Cervetto explains that red cedar is useful for smaller items such as hope chests and gun stocks but is too knotty for large lumber. Pine, on the other hand,

. . . is a valuable wood. Pine is used where it don't get wet. . . . Pine was used to frame a house, for floor beams, for ceiling, two-by-fours, rafters, but it also has to be covered away from dampness. Because the drier it gets, the harder it gets. For the outside wood they used cedar, for clapboard, cedar shingles. That withstood the weather a lot better than pine. All the old homes are built that way. Pine frame and covered with cedar.[7]

Many people in the Pinelands have built their own homes, including Cervetto.

Whether armed with an ax which he sharpens daily, as Cervetto does, or different sizes of chain saws, a woodsman will have to use the wind as another tool. "The main thing is that you got to catch the breeze," says Cervetto. "You see the wind controls them if the wind's blowing. That green top up there, if a little wind blows that, you couldn't hold it no how. I always watch that wind and then get to cutting where the wind helps you drop it where you want to."[8]

While today, independent woodsmen like Brewer and Cervetto feel that they make a comfortable living by combining lumbering with other seasonal work, in the nineteenth century, at least some of the woodsmen who worked for the owners of iron foundries felt less content. Their folksongs reflect their dissatisfaction with their lot in life. In 1937, John Youmans of Lakehurst sang "This Colliers Mill's a Very Fine Place" for folklorist Herbert Halpert. The song had been composed earlier by Rasher Moore of Colliers Mill to mock an owner who paid his workers in scrip money which was only good at the company store. In winter, when no work was available, he cut off credit at the store and made the workers either pay rent or vacate the company houses in which they lived. Sang Youmans:

> This Colliers Mill's a very fine place,
>   a sawmill and a store,
> And a hundred-acre cranberry bog
>   lie just before the door.
> As I went down to Colliers Mill,
>   the snow bein' very deep,
> As I went down to Colliers Mill
>   to get something for to eat.
> There I received a notice and plainly
>   it did say,
> "Vacate your house, old Rasher,
>   or I'll have you right away."[9]

Basketmaking

White oak (*Quercus alba*), which grows in the uplands, was used in the nineteenth century and in the first half of the twentieth century for basketmaking. There are two European-derived styles of traditional, wooden-splint baskets in the eastern United States. In the Adirondack Mountains and throughout New England, the splints were made by pounding ash logs to separate the yearly rings. Throughout the southern Appalachian Mountains, oak logs were split, and the splints were shaved on a shaving horse.

According to folklorist Henry Glassie, the occurrence of the pounded-ash and the split-oak traditions helps define the boundary between the southern and northern Appalachian Mountain culture areas.[10] The South Jersey baskets were in the split-oak tradition and were made in a variety of shapes and sizes, depending on their use. They included charcoal baskets, berry baskets, farm baskets, egg baskets, and eel traps. In the twentieth century, factory-made peach baskets began to replace the handmade, traditional baskets.

Perhaps the most famous basketmaker in the Pinelands was "Indian Ann," who lived near Indian Mills. She was said to be the daughter of a Delaware Indian named Ash Tamar or Elisha Moses Ashatama. Ashatama was indeed a Delaware Indian surname. The 1802 agreement to sell lands at

Clarence Morgan using splint-shaving horse. Courtesy of George H. Pierson, New Jersey Bureau of Forest Management, Division of Parks and Forestry.

the Brotherton Indian Reservation was signed by Elias Ashatama and Ann Ashatama, among others.[11]

"Indian Ann" married a man named Roberts. She was listed in the 1880 census as an Indian, age 87, whose occupation was basketmaking.[12] Her will, dated 1894, mentions that she had three sons and three daughters and that she owned a house and land in Shamong Township, Burlington County.[13] According to a local newspaper article dated 1932:

Indian Ann outlived her husband by many years and supported herself by making baskets which she sold in the neighborhood and in nearby towns. In summer she gathered blackberries and huckleberries and frequently walked as far as Vincentown, eleven miles distant, to sell them. She was a familiar figure in Vincentown and Medford, and many interesting anecdotes are told about her visits to these villages. She was usually accompanied by two small dogs, to which she was greatly attached.[14]

Opposite: *Clarence Morgan of Dividing Creek, basketmaker, 1944. Courtesy of George H. Pierson, New Jersey Bureau of Forest Management, Division of Parks and Forestry.*

Several local historical societies have baskets attributed to Indian Ann, and she is a popular figure as well in efforts to evoke the past. Indian Ann applehead dolls are made by residents and sold at festivities such as the Medford Apple Festival. Baskets that she is believed to have made also appear in decorative assemblages in area homes.

Charcoal Burning

The abundant pine of South Jersey woodlands was used to make charcoal, the fuel which, starting in the fourteenth century in Europe, was used in iron foundries. It also was used as the fuel in the New Jersey iron industry, and developed in the Pinelands along with that industry. After the decline of the iron industry here, charcoal was put to use as fuel for Delaware River steamboats and home furnaces in urban New Jersey.[15]

In the twentieth century, rural colliers had to compete with large commercial operations using brick kilns, but the small charcoalers continued to work in New Jersey until about 1970. In recent years, colliers Harry and Herbert Payne of Whiting made charcoal for a variety of users, including roofers who heated their tar pots with charcoal, restaurants that used it for

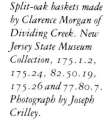

Split-oak baskets made by Clarence Morgan of Dividing Creek. New Jersey State Museum Collection, 175.1.2, 175.24, 82.50.19, 175.26 and 77.80.7. Photograph by Joseph Crilley.

"hearth" cooking, and local artists who used it for drawing. The brothers recalled to folklorist Mary Hufford that it "got to be quite an industry" in Whiting, where "you can't walk more than a half a mile in any direction without stumbling across evidence of an old kiln." During World War II, they sold much of their charcoal for use in the manufacture of gunpowder.[16]

In large-scale operations during the heyday of the industry, six to ten pits were often fired at the same time, spaced approximately 200 feet apart in an arrangement known as the "ring." A crew of men with specialized jobs were involved in the process: woodchoppers cut the cordwood; setters constructed the pits; scalpers placed the floats (pieces of turf) on top; blackers covered the floats with sand; firemen kept watch on the burning pits; drawers raked the floats off the pits; and teamsters transported the wood and charcoal.

These colliers often lived in temporary log cabins, known as "float cabins" because they were covered with floats and sand, like the charcoal pits. While the firing was underway, smaller lean-to structures, known as "watch

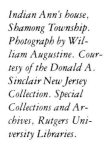

Indian Ann's house, Shamong Township. Photograph by William Augustine. Courtesy of the Donald A. Sinclair New Jersey Collection. Special Collections and Archives, Rutgers University Libraries.

A coaling site in the Pinelands, circa 1940. Courtesy of George H. Pierson, New Jersey Bureau of Forest Management, Division of Parks and Forestry.

Charcoal burning tools. Courtesy of George H. Pierson, New Jersey Bureau of Forest Management, Division of Parks and Forestry.

cabins," provided shelter and continuous visibility of the pit. Some of these watch cabins had handles so that they could be carried from one ring to another.[17]

Two types of pits were generally used in the Pinelands: the chimney pit and the arch pit. The pit was constructed in tiers around a "fagan," or guide pole, stuck vertically in the ground. In a chimney pit, the tiers were built around an interior triangular stack of cordwood that served as the chimney. In an arch pit, the wood was stacked in a V-formation with the fagan at the point, until the arch reached a height at which logs could be piled upright to form the first tier. When finished, the resulting pit had a side opening, or "arch," through which it could be fired and additional kindling in-serted. This was also called a "female" pit, presumably in contrast to the chimney pit.

The second step was "turfing and blacking." It involved covering the pit four to five inches deep with "floats" of turf, which were usually cut from sandy soil containing sheep laurel, black huckleberry, and teaberry. Then

the pit was "blacked" by covering it with a four- to six-inch-deep layer of sand which formed an airtight seal.

To "fire the pit," kindling was inserted in the chimney or through the arch and set afire. Then the chimney or arch was filled with two-foot lengths of cordwood and covered with floats and sand. Flue holes were then punched through the floats and sand about one foot apart and one to two feet above the base of the pit. By covering and opening these flue holes, the collier could control the speed and evenness of the charring process. Too much air caused the wood to decompose into gases, vapors, and solids, leaving only ashes instead of charcoal.

It took eight to ten days to burn an eight-cord pit. Many pits burned for as long as two weeks, during which time they had to be watched night and day. The collier could monitor the burn from the appearance of the smoke. If white steam came out of the flue holes, the wood was being carbonized properly. But if blue smoke emerged, the wood was burning, and a "soft spot" would develop where the wood caught fire and burned a hole. In this

A burning charcoal pit, circa 1940. Courtesy of George H. Pierson, New Jersey Bureau of Forest Management, Division of Parks and Forestry.

Bagging the charcoal. Courtesy of George H. Pierson, New Jersey Bureau of Forest Management, Division of Parks and Forestry.

case, the soft spot had to be "dressed" immediately by cleaning it out, filling it with chunk wood, and covering it with new floats and sand.

After the pit had slowly burned for eight to fourteen days, it would settle, and sand would sift unevenly down through the pit. The fire had "come to foot" when the pit finished settling. It would then be "keeled" by closing the flue holes and turning the floats so that sand would sift down and the pit would cool. Finally, the pit was "drawn" when the turf and sand were raked off. The cooled charcoal was then raked into a ring, and the "braise," or charred bark, was flaked off and left in the pit. The large chunks, known as "ring coal," were broken into smaller sizes. The charcoal was then loaded into boxes or sacks.[18]

An entry of July 1812 from the *Martha Furnace Diary and Journal* reflects this scene:

22. Joseph Camp carting floats in coaling with three horses.

23. Camp continues coaling. Abbot and Sermon ariv. last evening.

Cranberry label. Photograph by Anthony Masso.

*Birds-eye view of Egg
Harbor City, 1865.
Lent by the New Jersey
Historical Society.
Photograph of litho-
graph by Anthony
Masso.*

A Pinelands Mosaic.
Photograph by Joseph
Czarnecki. PFP 83–
CJC045–A/3.

Blueberry Packing
House. Painting by
Margaret Bakely of
Vincentown. Photo-
graph by Anthony
Masso.

Roadside stand, New Egypt. Photograph by Joseph Czarnecki. PFP 83–JC009–5.

Bill Wasiowich of Woodmansie. Photograph by Joseph Czarnecki. PFP 83–CJC016–07.

Bucci Farm Market,
Highway 40. Photo-
graph by Elaine
Thatcher. PFP 83–
CET007–17.

Grave blanket, Egg
Harbor City Cemetery.
Photograph by Susan
Samuelson. American
Folklife Center, PFP
83–CSS047–19.

*Railbird hunting on
the Maurice River.
Photograph by Dennis
McDonald. PFP 84–
CDM030–18.*

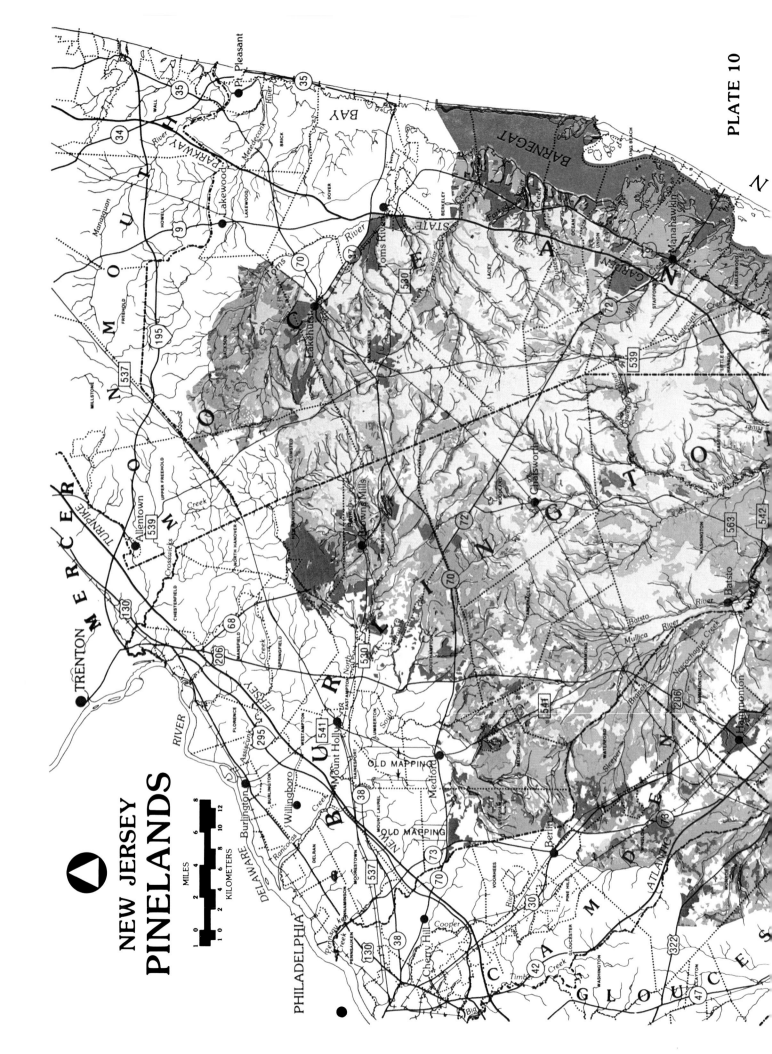

NEW JERSEY PINELANDS

MILES

KILOMETERS

PLATE 10

N

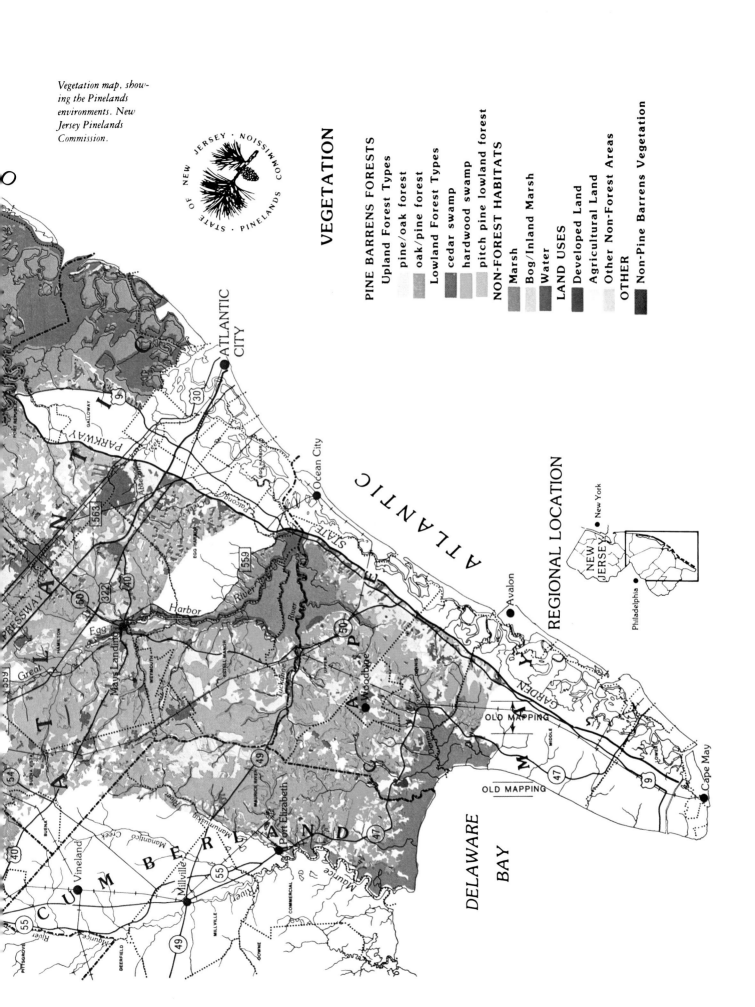

Vegetation map, showing the Pinelands environments. New Jersey Pinelands Commission.

STATE OF NEW JERSEY · PINELANDS COMMISSION

VEGETATION

PINE BARRENS FORESTS
Upland Forest Types
- pine/oak forest
- oak/pine forest

Lowland Forest Types
- cedar swamp
- hardwood swamp
- pitch pine lowland forest

NON-FOREST HABITATS
- Marsh
- Bog/Inland Marsh
- Water

LAND USES
- Developed Land
- Agricultural Land
- Other Non-Forest Areas

OTHER
- Non-Pine Barrens Vegetation

REGIONAL LOCATION

New York
NEW JERSEY
Philadelphia

ATLANTIC CITY

Ocean City

ATLANTIC

Avalon

Cape May

DELAWARE BAY

OLD MAPPING

OLD MAPPING

GARDEN STATE

Vineland

Millville

CUMBERLAND

Mays Landing

Egg Harbor

Port Elizabeth

Woodbine

Cranberries floating in a flooded bog, Haines and Haines cranberry bog, Hog Wallow. Photograph by Susan Samuelson. PFP 83 – CSSD05 – 12.

*A row of beating ma-
chines in a flooded
cranberry bog, Hog
Wallow. Photograph by
Joseph Czarnecki. PFP
83–JC004–5.*

*Beating machines in
action, Hog Wallow.
Photograph by Joseph
Czarnecki. PFP 83–
CJC004–13.*

*Cranberries being
loaded by a conveyor
belt onto carts for
transportation to the
packing house, Hog
Wallow. Photograph by
Joseph Czarnecki. PFP
83–JC005–12.*

Pair of merganser de-
coys by Hurley Conklin
of Manahawkin. New
Jersey State Museum.
83.64.1,2. Photo-
graph by Anthony
Masso.

Glass items made by
Ted Ramp of Egg Har-
bor City. Photograph
by Anthony Masso.

Batsto. Painting by
Win Salmons of New
Gretna. Lent by Anne
Salmons. Photograph
by Anthony Masso.

Cranberry Reservoir. *Painting by Margaret Bakely of Vincentown. Photograph by Anthony Masso.*

Picking Cranberries at Peterson's Bog. *Painting by Bluma Bayuk Rappoport Purmell. Lent by Michèle Rappoport. Photograph by Anthony Masso.*

Signature quilt in the tumbling block pattern made by the Sew and Sews of the Tabernacle Methodist Church. Lent by the Tabernacle Historical Society. Photograph by Dennis McDonald.

24. ditto ditto ditto Job Mathis has gone to Tuckerton.

25. ditto ditto ditto All going well. Friend Pedler arrived here last evening with books and skins of various kinds.

27. Thomas Anderson drunk. Craig on turn all night.

28. All going on well. Steward carting logs for I. Cramer. Camp in the coaling.

29. Camp carting floats for Patrick Hamilton.

30. Garner Crane went home at noon on account of his wife being indisposed. Camp in the coaling.

31. Camp carting floats in the coaling.[19]

Individual colliers modified the process of charcoal burning. Herbert Payne, who "coaled" until 1974, experimented with both materials and methods. He developed his own personal technique by combining the chimney and arch pits. In order to meet a demand for extra-hot charcoal, he began using old railroad ties. He found that the ties from the defunct Tuckerton Railroad worked best, so that he eventually could claim that he'd turned the whole Tuckerton Railroad into charcoal!

Payne recalled that in the old days, the "firewalker" would walk on the pit as it smoldered, packing soft spots so that the wood would smolder evenly. On one occasion, Payne burned his leg while firewalking, but his skill in judging the burn eventually became so great that he was able to moonlight at another job in Toms River while his pit was smoldering in Whiting.[20]

Ironmaking

According to historian John Stilgoe, from the time of the Middle Ages, mines and furnaces were associated in the European folk mentality with Satan and Hell. The "husbandman," or farmer, on the other hand, was associated with the positive values of hearth and home. Such attitudes did not interfere with commerce, however. The farmers bought the stoves, plows, skillets, and hoes that rural blacksmiths made from the products of the furnace.[21]

Attitudes derived from such ancient European roots may be implicated in regional prejudices. Many of the people who settled in the Pinelands in the 1800s were employed in the iron industry with its blazing furnaces, and so may have been regarded suspiciously by those outside the Pines. This bias, then, may have contributed to the stereotype of Pinelanders that survived long after the demise of the iron furnaces in the mid-nineteenth century.

The South Jersey iron industry began about 1765. It drew not only upon the bog iron, or limonite, found in the swamps along the streams of the Pinelands, but also upon the available water for power, the extensive woodlands for charcoal, the sandy soil for castings and insulation, and the lime in oyster shells found along the rivers and bays for smelting. The main products of the furnaces and forges were munitions, and cast-iron stoves, pots, pans, axe heads, shovels, and water pipes.

The iron ore was dug up and transported in large ore boats to the furnace. First, the ore had to be prepared in the "stamping mill," where large, water-powered trip hammers crushed it into smaller particles. Then the ore was roasted (by placing the ore on a grate and igniting a fire under it) to remove excess water and to convert any carbonates or sulfides into ferric oxide.

The smelting process required a flux and a reducing agent. In South Jersey, the flux was usually lime (in the form of oyster shells), which combined with the impurities in the iron to form slag. The reducing agent was carbon (in the form of charcoal), which combined with the oxide in the iron oxide to form carbon monoxide.

Small iron fireplace kettle, Allaire Iron Works (Howell) Monmouth County, 1823– 1846. New Jersey State Museum Collection, 77.80.6. Photograph by Joseph Crilley.

A fire was kindled in the hearth until the stack was thoroughly heated. The batch of ore, flux, and charcoal combined in specific proportions was transported in wheelbarrows over a trestle bridge to a platform around the top of the furnace and dumped into the top of the stack in layers. Blasts of cold air kept the molten mass in a state of agitation and provided oxygen to complete the combustion. As the mass melted, the slag floated to the top and the purified metal sank to the bottom. The slag was drawn off periodically, and the iron drawn out every nine to ten hours.

Forges usually were located near the furnaces. The forge refined and re-smelted the pig iron into malleable wrought iron, or "bar iron." Pig iron had limited use as stoves, hollow ware, kettles, sash weights, and firebacks; wrought iron could be made into such items as tools, horseshoes, and wagon tires.

At the forge, the pig iron was reheated in a blast fire and pounded by

Howell Iron Works, Monmouth County, circa 1850. Courtesy of the Monmouth County Historical Association.

HOWELL FURNACE.

heavy, water-powered hammers into bars called "anconies." Some furnaces combined the operations of forge and furnace. Some ironworks also had "rolling mills" that made sheet iron, and "slitting mills" that made iron rods, nails, and tires for wagon wheels.

The production of iron in the late eighteenth century was a rural industry, but it required considerable capital and a large workforce. Most of the "iron masters," such as Charles Read, Isaac Potts, John Cox, and William Richards, were wealthy men, but they required sometimes two or more partners to raise the required capital.

Around the forge or furnace was a village usually consisting of the iron master's mansion, the workers' houses, a sawmill, a gristmill, a store, a school, a church, and sometimes a stamping mill. Martha Furnace, for example, founded in 1793 by Isaac Potts, had 40 to 50 structures and a population of 400 in its heyday.

Iron fireback set, Atsion Furnace, Burlington County, 1790–1840. New Jersey State Museum Collection, 72.129a, b,c. Photograph by Joseph Crilley.

Iron plantations required a workforce that included founders; fillers or bankmen, who loaded the furnace; guttermen and molders, who handled the molten metal; and blacksmiths and patternmakers. In addition, there were workers outside the furnace, including "ore raisers," who dug the ore out of the bogs, charcoal burners, lumbermen, and teamsters, who hauled

the raw materials to the furnace and the finished product to nearby river landings.[22]

The furnaces operated 24 hours a day continuously from spring to December or January. Some of the forge workers were slaves, but most were white, indentured servants who agreed to work for a specified number of years. Nevertheless, it was not uncommon for them to run away.

The entries from the *Martha Furnace Diary and Journal* reflect the round of activities associated with the iron industry:

April 1808

26. John Lynch helping P. Applegate about the furnace wheel. S. Stewart hauled 6 loads Ore from the Pond.

27. Commenced hauling coal. Owen Hedger driving John Hedgers Team. Stewart hauling sand to Furnace. . . .

29. . . . Peter Cox began to fill the furnace.

30. At 11 o'clock A.M. put the Furnace in Blast. Asa Lanning filled 1 turn. J. Hedger Banksman. John Cunning doing Gutterman's duty. . . .

November 1808

5. John Bodines Team hauled 1 Ld. Shells & ½ Ton Iron. Luker hauled Logs in forenoon. Stewart Cuttg. Logs.

6. J. Bodines Team hauled 2 Lds. Hay & 1 Ton stoves. Isaac Cramers Team hauled wood to Ventling.

7. Forenoon. Hauled 2 Tons Stoves in afternoon. . . .

April 1809

20. At 25 M past 2 o'clock P.M. put the Furnace in Blast. Delaney & Cox Fillers. Hedger putting up the Ore & Donaghou Banksman. Ventling & Townsend working in the Blacksmiths Shop.

21. Teams hauled Moulding sand in forenoon (Bennett & Brown). Ventling ½ day in Blksmh. Shop. . . .

22. Teams hauling from Gravelly Point. King & Cos. Team hauled Mdg. Sand in the afternoon. Albertus King arrived from Philadelphia.

23. The furnace working well. . . .

July 1812

15. Craig & Anderson filling up the furnace with coal.

16. Furnace went some time last night. . . .

17. All hands at their usual business.

18. Teams carting moulding sand. . . .

20. Furnace made a great puff on Sunday night last, but fortunately done no damage.[23]

In the mid-nineteenth century, the South Jersey iron industry declined. Experts disagree on the reasons for this decline, but one factor was that the ore began to be depleted and furnaces such as Batsto had to import ore from other places. Also, the discovery of anthracite coal near the magnetite, or rock iron, ore in Pennsylvania—coupled with the development of the hot-blast method—made the charcoal, limonite, cold-blast complex of South Jersey obsolete. Because of its high phosphorous content, bog iron could not be used to make steel.

The history of Batsto Furnace illustrates the rise and fall of the iron industry. Located near the site of a sawmill on Batsto Creek, a tributary of the Mullica River, Batsto was built in 1766 by Charles Read and his business associates, who also built forges and furnaces at Etna, Taunton, and Atsion. Under Read's ownership the principal product of Batsto was pig iron, some of which was transported to the forge at Atsion to be refined into bar iron.

At the time of the Revolutionary War, Batsto was owned by John Cox, a Philadelphia merchant, and his associates. Cox expanded the furnace's products to include pots, kettles, Dutch ovens, skillets, stoves, mortars and pestles, sash weights, forge hammers, and evaporating pans for salt works. Batsto also made cannon balls for the Continental Army.

In 1778 Batsto was purchased by Joseph Ball, who had been the manager of the works under Cox and his partners. Ball constructed a forge and slitting mill about half a mile from the furnace. In 1784 Ball and his partners sold Batsto to William Richards and his associates. Richards rebuilt the furnace.

Batsto flourished under the ownership of William Richards's son, Jesse Richards, and his partners. The principal reason for the boom was the demand for munitions during the War of 1812. During the 1840s Batsto had two sawmills and a brick factory; its products included pipe, ornamental iron, and firebacks. In 1841 Jesse Richards built a "cupola," or resmelting furnace, that refined pig iron into products of higher quality.

When nearby iron ore began to be depleted, Richards imported ore from New York and Pennsylvania. As the iron industry in New Jersey began to decline, Richards decided to diversify. In 1846 he built a factory to make window glass. A second glassworks was also built, but the two were not successful.[24]

Over the latter half of the nineteenth century, Philadelphian Joseph Wharton purchased the Batsto mansion and more than 100,000 acres of Richards's land. He planned to divert the region's abundant water supply to Philadelphia. In 1884 the New Jersey state legislature thwarted his plan, but over the next 75 years, the area continued to be the target of development proposals. During the 1950s the state purchased the Wharton tract, and began restoration of the village soon after.

Today, as a state historic site, Batsto encompasses reconstructed operating mills, workers' houses, and a nature center; various programs interpret the relationship between culture and nature. Even the sight of unrestored ruins can powerfully evoke the past. Such an encounter seems to have taken place as early as 1823, when the traveler J. F. Watson wrote:

> Was much interested to see the formidable ruins at Atsion iron works. They looked as picturesque as the ruins of abbeys, etc., in pictures. There were dams, forges, furnaces, storehouses, a dozen houses and lots for the workmen, and the whole comprising a town; a place once overwhelming the ear with the din of unceasing, ponderous hammers, or alarming the sight with fire and smoke, and smutty and sweating Vulcans. Now all is hushed, no wheels turn, no fires blaze, the houses are unroofed, and the frames, etc., have fallen down and not a foot of the busy workmen is seen.[25]

Reconstructed villages such as Batsto and Allaire, the site of the old Howell Iron Works, make the past accessible to visitors and residents alike, just as do the re-enactments of historical events that take place in costume and pageantry at local festivals.[26]

The element of personal history that connects place and past may be the impetus for formal expressions of sense of place. The families of artist Win Salmons and his widow, Anne, lived in the New Gretna area for generations. Salmons's paintings depict the multiple connections between their lives and the Pinelands. Mrs. Salmons's grandparents were caretakers of the Batsto mansion for years. Win, she recalls, loved to go up and sketch scenes, and through some of his paintings she unravels the thread of the personal past that is woven into public history. Of Salmons's painting of the Batsto mansion, she explains:

> This is a picture that is of the Wharton tract. It's the Batsto mansion. My grandfather and grandmother lived here till just before the state bought

The Pines. *Painting by Win Salmons of New Gretna. Photograph by Anthony Masso.*

it in '54. In fact, they stayed right here in this room which is the oldest part of the mansion, see? This part was built first by Read.[27]

Another of Salmons's paintings, depicting a clearing in the Pines, prompts her to recall special encounters with nature:

> We used to talk when we'd like pick up things to make wreaths. You know—for Christmas for cemeteries and things. The Pines sing, you know. They just kind of sing. It's like we—most everybody knows— around here. You can tell there's going to be a storm. They sigh. It's like a pretty music in the trees.[28]

Iron forges have long provided the context for verbal genres in the Pines, as well. In the late 1930s and early 1940s, folklorist Herbert Halpert collected a cycle of stories about a wizard or magician named Jerry Munyhun. Many of these stories were centered on Old Hanover Furnace and its vicinity. No one knew where Munyhun originated, or even whether he really lived. Some people thought Munyhun was Irish, others thought he was black, and still others called him "the Old Hanover Hessian." Harry Payne recalls his father talking about Munyhun:

Was an old fellow from down at Waretown, fellow by the name of Acton Bunnel. He was a fisherman. . . . He was tellin' about Jerry Munyhun. Said that Jerry had sold his soul to the devil so that he would have unusual powers over other human beings. He was a man about my father's age, and I guess Pop met him through buying salt hay for his horses. Once in awhile he'd come by and he'd sit down and talk and have dinner together. He'd say "Charlie, remember old Jerry Munyhun? Remember?" Pop'd say, "Yeah, I heard about him," and tell the story all over again.[29]

Munyhun, it was said, could stop a person in his tracks and chop large amounts of wood by making the axe do the work. He could turn oyster shells into money or hogs into corn cobs. He could not be shot or held in jail.

On June 26, 1941, George White of Lakehurst told the following Munyhun tale to Halpert:

Jerry Munahun—not Monahan. My father-in-law, Tom Luker, used to tell us these yarns about him. They told it for the fact. He worked at Old Hanover Furnace—and they owed him quite some money. So, they wouldn't pay him; so they couldn't do anything with their plant— couldn't get no steam with their boilers. And he went away and was gone awhile. And he come back again. And he asked them what the trouble was—and they said they didn't know. Couldn't get no steam; couldn't make the fire burn. And he told them he knowed what the trouble was. He says, "If you pay me, they'll all fly out." Which they paid him, and they did—went out. They claimed they flew out of there one after the other. That's the way he made it look to them. They told that for the truth. These real old people, I've had more than one tell me these things he done. They claimed he was a great man.[30]

Papermaking

With the decline of the iron industry, other uses were found for the resources left by the numerous ironworks. These resources included mills and lakes which could be used for other manufacturing processes.

In 1832, William McCarty bought the forge and slitting mill that had been built in 1795 by Isaac Potts on the Wading River near the site of Harris-

South Jersey wagon in front of the Harrisville paper factory. William Augustine Collection, Donald A. Sinclair New Jersey Collection. Special Collections and Archives, Rutgers University Libraries.

ville. The Wading River Forge and Slitting Mill had used pig iron from nearby Martha Furnace, which Potts had also owned.

McCarty renamed the place McCartyville and decided to make paper rather than iron. He enlarged the slitting mill dam and constructed a system of canals and millraces. By 1835, McCarty had in operation a double paper mill, with one mill manufacturing nearly a ton of paper a day.

In 1851 William D. and Richard C. Harris bought the property and renamed it Harrisville. They expanded the paper mill, enlarged the canals, and built a gas plant to supply the factory and village. The main product at Harrisville was a thick, heavy, brown paper known as "butcher's paper." Despite attempts to get the Raritan and Delaware Railroad (later the New Jersey Central) to build a line to Harrisville, the railroad was built eight miles to the west, leading to the demise of the papermaking operation at Harrisville.

The raw materials for papermaking included old rags, rope, scrap paper, bagging, and salt hay. The salt hay was harvested at nearby marshes and transported in wagons to the factory. The other raw materials were shipped from Philadelphia or New York.[31]

Glassmaking

Glassmaking began in South Jersey in 1739, when Caspar Wistar built a glasshouse on Alloways Creek in Salem County. He imported experienced German glassblowers. While most of the early South Jersey glass factories were outside the boundaries of the Pinelands, in the nineteenth century there were more than 20 glasshouses in the Pines. Most of these factories made bottles and window glass; a few made cut glass and tableware.

The Pinelands offered many resources to Wistar and the glassmakers who followed him. Glass was made from a "batch" consisting of silica, lime, and soda which had been mixed with broken glass. Silica was available in the sandy soil of the Pinelands. The lime came from limestone brought from Staten Island and Valley Forge. The soda was also imported from outside the region. The furnaces were fueled by cordwood, which was readily available in the Pines. Salt hay was used for packing.

In the nineteenth century, hollow ware factories were those which pro-

Sand pits owned by Samuel Hilliard, on the Maurice River near Millville, circa 1876. From New Historical Atlas of Cumberland County, New Jersey. *Philadelphia: D. J. Stewart, 1876.*

Interior of the Star Glass Works, Medford, circa 1910. Courtesy of Everett Mickle and the Medford Historical Society.

duced bottles. They were divided into "shops." A shop was a group of men working around a single "glory hole" (opening in the furnace). Each shop consisted of a gatherer, a blower, or "gaffer," and sometimes a finisher. There were also helpers called "boys." The gatherer placed the head of the blowpipe into a pot of molten glass, called the "metal." He worked the metal into an elongated ball, and he "marvered," or flattened, it on a flat plate to remove impurities and to consolidate the mass. The blower then placed this mixture, called a "parison," into a wooden mold and blew

through the blowpipe to form the desired shape. Next, the finisher took it to the gaffer's bench, where he placed a pontil rod on the bottom of the bottle and broke off the blowpipe. The gatherer then brought a small amount of metal to the finisher, who attached it to the neck and then shaped the top and the lip. Once the bottle was finished, it was placed in a lehr to cool gradually. In the first decade of the twentieth century, an automatic bottle-blowing machine was introduced, making the earlier method obsolete.

There were two methods for making windowlight. The earliest was known as the crown method. The blower took a pear-shaped globule of melted glass from the oven and twirled it into a disk about 36 inches in diameter. After it was cooled in an annealing oven, small panes were cut from the disks. Most of the windowpanes made in New Jersey, however, were produced by the cylinder method. The gatherer gathered 80 to 100 pounds of melted glass in two or three stages and turned it into a hemispherical shape. Then the blower blew the glass into a balloon shape several feet long and took it to a pit. Swinging his blowpipe like a pendulum, the blower stretched the glass into a six-foot length. After the glass was cooled, the ends were cracked off, leaving a glass cylinder which was grooved, split, and then flattened into sheets which were cut into windowpanes.

Around the turn of the twentieth century, machines were developed that could draw out flat sheets of glass, thus making the cylinder method obsolete. New Jersey factories did not adopt this new technology and instead ceased to produce windowlight.[32]

Lampwork, also known as flameworking, torch working, or scientific glassblowing, has been used in factories since the late nineteenth century to make laboratory apparatus. A glass rod or tubing is manipulated in the intense heat of a small burner to the desired shape. Glassworkers have used the same technique to make their own folk objects, such as toys and miniatures.

According to former lamproom blower Dorothy Lilly, "If you grew up in Millville, you were raised on glass."[33] The statement could be applied as well to towns of the Pinelands whose economies and societies were shaped and sustained by glasshouses. A glass factory required a wide range of auxiliary industries, including sand mining, woodcutting, and potmaking. Within the glasshouse itself were many shops filling different needs: mold shops, art shops, cutting and grinding shops, and packing shops. Therefore, a sizable population could be sustained by a few factories.

The annual cycle in these towns revolved around the fiery furnaces of the glasshouse. In the summer, they would shut down. Lilly, whose grandparents and parents worked in the industry, recalls that her family would go to Wildwood for the summer, where her father worked as a trolley conductor.[34]

Social hierarchies were established according to occupational hierarchies. Glassblowers were well paid and always in demand. They often became a social elite within the town as a result.

Many families counted many members and several generations among glasshouse employees. Lilly's grandparents, parents, and husband all worked in glass. Women often did decorative work and packing in the factories. Family members passed on skills in formal and informal ways. Malcolm Jones, whose father, like himself, was a moldmaker, recalls that it was difficult to get an apprenticeship in the mold shop unless one had a relative there.[35] Lilly began learning in a less formal way. She would take lunch to her father, who would let her try to blow a gather on his blowpipe. She quickly learned that if she blew too fast, the glass would burst and scatter "blovers" around the shop. During World War II, Lilly developed her skills further doing lamproom blowing at the Frederick Dimmick plant.[36]

Within the many shops of the glasshouse, communities of workers developed their own cycles, hierarchies, and customs. The more skilled craftsmen had to go through an apprenticeship of up to five years. A young boy might begin his apprenticeship as young as age 12. During the years until he was "out of his time," as completion of apprenticeship was called, he would work at many tasks within the shop, and learn by observation as well as by practice. In the moldmaking shop, an apprentice would be as-

Left: *Engraved vase and decanter. Lent by Dorothy Lilly. Photograph by Anthony Masso.*

Right: *Engraved vase made from a chemical beaker by Walter Earling of Millville. Lent by Walter Earling. Photograph by Michael Bergman.*

signed either to the machine or to the bench in his third year. The latter spot was much coveted, for it meant that he would become a letter cutter, the highest paid and most skilled man in the shop. A letter cutter would do the fine handwork, such as carving letters or designs in the iron mold after the machine work had been completed.

Apprentices quickly learned the physics of glassmaking with some traditional pranks. Ted Ramp recalls, "You'd blow a long piece of glass, like a tube, and pinch it shut, and that air'd get so hot in there, it would blow all to pieces."[37] In his reminiscences of the glasshouse in *Tempo: The Glass Folks of South Jersey,* Roy C. Horner recalls similar items called "snappers," "Dutch tears," or "Prince Rupert's drops" that were formed by dropping molten glass into a bucket of water. The glass would harden into a tear-shaped drop with a tail. When a wily journeyman would place the snapper in the hand of the apprentice and quickly snap off the tail, it would explode into fine dust.[38]

More pleasant traditions often drew on the materials in the shop and the special skills of the workers. In the glasscutting shops of the Whitall–Tatum factory, it was traditional to present each girl in the art shop with an

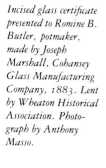

Incised glass certificate presented to Romine B. Butler, potmaker, made by Joseph Marshall, Cohansey Glass Manufacturing Company, 1883. Lent by Wheaton Historical Association. Photograph by Anthony Masso.

engraved decanter or vase on her sixteenth birthday. In Lilly's family, there are two of these. One is a decanter engraved with an "E," which was presented to her grandmother, Ella Estlow, around 1880. The other is a vase, created from a chemical beaker by cutting the top off and polishing the edge, which is engraved with "Hazel B. Estlow," and which was presented to Lilly's mother.[39]

Apparently, in some shops a certificate was presented on the completion of apprenticeship. At the Museum of American Glass at Historic Wheaton Village in Millville, an elaborately engraved pane of glass commemorates that occasion for Romine B. Butler, who "served his full apprenticeship for the art of potmaking at Cohansey Glass Manufacturing Company of Bridgeton." The certificate was engraved by Joseph Marshall in June 1883.

Glasscutter Walter Earling recalls other items that he and other cutters and grinders made both to hone skills and to create "whimsies," as such folk art is often called. Earling once ground lapidary cuts onto a glass doorknob, then mounted it on a base. Dentists' dapping dishes became salt cellars by such a process, and he once engraved his name and a sampler of designs on a chemical beaker to create a vase.[40]

South Jersey jar, made by the Moore Brothers Glass Company, Clayton, circa 1870. New Jersey State Museum Collection, 324. Photograph by Joseph Crilley.

Much of this was done before and after work or during breaks, and has come to be called "end of day" work or "tempo" work. It often went home for use as sugar bowls, pitchers, rolling pins, and vases. Other items were used decoratively, such as chains, batons, canes, hats, lilies, knitting needles, button hooks, Christmas ornaments, and paperweights.[41]

The paperweight became an important emblem of skill among glass-workers. While some were made using a metal die, they were not mass produced here. In southern New Jersey, characteristic shapes became localized in such designs as the "Millville Rose." The men who perfected these designs, such as Ralph Barber and Emil Larsen, were highly regarded, and the items eagerly sought after. Yet, glassblowers were never allowed to make paperweights on company time because they were not a profitable product for the factory. Most glassblowers at one time or another tested their skills by making paperweights. Often they incorporated into the designs the traditional community values of home, church, and country.

Many glassworkers took the skills they had acquired in the large factories

Ted Ramp's son, William, closes the wooden mold, which has been soaked previously in water, around the ribbed parison, while Ted rotates the blowpipe and blows into it to inflate the bulbous base of the vessel, 1970. Photograph by William Augustine. Donald A. Sinclair New Jersey Collection. Special Collections and Archives, Rutgers University Libraries.

and began their own small shops. Among these were the Clevengers, whose family involvement in glass reached back to Batsto, and Ted Ramp, whose occupational and familial roots are German.

William Clevenger worked in the windowlight furnace at Batsto between 1844 and 1866. When the Batsto works declined, he moved to Clayton to work in the Moore Brothers' glass factory; his sons, Thomas (Tommy), Lorenzo (Reno), and William Elbert (Allie), went to work in the factory also. When the Moore factory closed down just before World War I, the Clevengers, like other glassworkers, had to resort to odd jobs.

According to a South Jersey antiques expert named Ernest C. Stanmire, he accompanied the Clevenger brothers to the 1926 Sesquicentennial Exposition in Philadelphia, where they saw the original log cabin Booz bottles made by the Whitney Glass Works being sold as collectibles. With money borrowed from Stanmire, the Clevengers built a one-pot furnace and began producing handblown glass. Many collectors consider their glass to be "reproductions" of colonial glass to supply the fashionable Colonial Revival

William Ramp holds small amount of molten glass to the vessel now affixed to a pontil rod, while Ted, using shears, guides its application to form a handle, 1970. Photograph by William Augustine. Donald A. Sinclair New Jersey Collection. Special Collections and Archives, Rutgers University Libraries.

market of the 1920s. But they can also be considered as reviving the folk tradition of "free-blown" glass that was on the verge of dying out.

Allie Clevenger continued to blow glass until his death in 1960. The Clevenger Works continues today under the proprietorship of James Travis, Jr.

Ted Ramp of Egg Harbor City recalls that "old man Larsen was a dandy" when it came to making paperweights. Larsen was one of the many glass-blowers with whom Ted worked over his long career.

Ramp began working as a gathering boy at the Liberty Cut Glass Works in Egg Harbor. He eventually worked as a gaffer in shops throughout South Jersey and in West Virginia, as well as in the shop he ran behind his own home for approximately 15 years.

Ramp's years at the Hofbauer glass factory in Vineland had a great impact on his work. Hofbauer came from Austria, opened his factory in 1932, and produced art glass that was sold through department stores like Gimbels. While he worked there, Ted acquired many of the stylistic traits which continued to characterize his work, including crimped edges, optical effects, and swirled and fluted motifs.

But the moldmaking that Ramp learned at Hofbauer's may have been as important as anything else he learned there. As he tells it:

Hofbauer made the wooden molds himself, and I'm watching him, and he said, "You think you could do that?" And I said, "Yeah, maybe a little

Glass pitcher made by Ted Ramp of Egg Harbor City. Lent by Helen Zimmer. Photograph by Anthony Masso.

better than you." He'd cut a piece of wood, round like that, take an axe and split it. And you know how rough everything is and that's why I told him. He throwed a hatchet at me! He was a crazy Dutchman! . . . It took me all day to make [my first mold]. You had to chip it out by hand, you know, on a gouge. And then he give me hell why didn't I tell him I could make it before! I made prit' near all his molds after that.[42]

He cut cherry and apple trees and carved the molds out in his basement for five dollars each.

These handmade molds became a hallmark of Ramp's own work, for few people were using wooden molds by that time. He also made molds for other factories later, including Clevenger Brothers and Wheaton.

While Ramp ran his own shop behind his house, he was working full time elsewhere. He would start the oven up on Thursday evening and stay up all weekend blowing glass and tending the fire so that the "batch" wouldn't be ruined. Customers would arrive by five in the morning, his wife recalls; she had to hide pieces she wanted to keep! His younger son, and later his granddaughter, sometimes helped him in the shop.

Most of Ramp's work is in amber, amethyst, cobalt, green, or bluestone. He would create optical effects by first blowing the gather into wire, then finishing it in a wooden mold. Stripes were applied on hot glass in the following manner: "When you got the hot glass—that was white. You stick that on the pipe and hold it there till it starts to melt, then you twist it— twist it around. And then you take a pair of pincers and pull the color up."[43] Though he made many pitchers and vases, it is the small, fluted basket that is distinctively "Ramp glass."

Hunting, Trapping, and Gathering

With the decline of great industries in the Pines in the late nineteenth century, much of the landscape which had bustled with activity for a century reverted to wilderness. This change coincided with changes in the general perception of wilderness.

Geographer Yi Fu Tuan points out that in the late nineteenth century, under the influence of the conservation movement, the wilderness began gaining value as an "edenic" retreat from the chaos of the city. Twentieth-century values and views of the wilderness as threatened by development have reinforced this notion.[44] Recreational uses and suburban settlements have resulted from it.

Opposite: *Harmony Gun Club. Photograph by Mary Hufford. PFP218973–1–25.*

Many of the members of the innumerable Pinelands hunting clubs view that environment as a kind of ritual homeland where men gather to share each other's company and to forget the rigors of modern life in the city.

In 1980, there were more than 300 such clubs in the Pines, most of them maintained by men living outside the area. Many of the groups first formed their clubs and built their lodges in the 1920s. Membership usually reflects family and occupational networks. Members may use a lodge for fishing or family events, but its main function is to house the group during the week-long annual deer hunt in December.

While the week in the woods is a ritual itself, it also serves as a frame for many other carefully constructed and observed customs. Typically, club members arrive several days before the season opens to prepare the lodge, the woods, and themselves. Some members scout the woods to identify recent deer movement and to plan the hunt. On the Sunday of deer week, each club has a party and members of different clubs visit each other in a formal and congenial recognition of their shared space in the woods. This is honored as well in the structure of the hunt. The "woods captain" of each club has a "woods schedule" which reflects the silent agreement among the clubs to manage shared space equitably: "You don't push onto us and we won't push onto you." [45] During a hunt, some club members will "drive," that is, move in a tight line through the woods to flush the deer, and others will "stand" a good distance upwind of the drivers to shoot deer that run by.

Traditionally, a hunter who misses a shot will have his shirttails cut off. Mementos of such infamy are tacked on walls, framed in pictures, and chartered into "shirttail clubs." At the annual banquet held after the deer season, most clubs re-enact or satirize particular events of the year's hunt.

While most club members live outside the Pinelands, their long years of association with the region and the natives, as well as their caretaker attitudes towards the woods, usually earn them a special "resident nonresident" status. Much of the hunting is done on privately held lands by agreement with the owners. Natives often regard hunting as a form of deer population control that benefits them personally, and club members are generally careful to safeguard the owner's property as they hunt. Reciprocally, natives watch over the hunting lodges, which are targets for vandalism by "outsiders." [46]

Even for the man who hasn't gotten a deer in nine years, the challenge of the hunt and the camaraderie of the club make the hunting lodge a regenerative woodland shelter. According to one: "You're down here for a week; it is another world. No cars, no nothing. And you don't realize there's cars until you get up to the White Horse Pike, and then it's the old hubbub again." [47]

Like many other Pinelands woodsmen, Jack Cervetto has guided hunters for many years. Hunter guiding serves as an important link in two chains of activity. With their knowledge of place, native guides map the otherwise indecipherable environment for visitors, helping them use the area as a recreational resource. On the other hand, guiding itself is an important occupational resource for men who "work the cycle."

> I used to take deer parties, big clubs, out here years ago for deer season. At one time, I had thirty, forty men. Put thirty of 'em on a stand and ten for drivers. Sometimes you have twelve drivers. It all depends on the bottom, how you can see. If it's thick bottom, you have to get closer together. If it's open bottom, you'd take less. And my drives were already laid out on paper, you know, from one drive to the other, and eventually the boys got to know the drives, too.[48]

Knowing the life cycles, habits, and habitats of the flora and fauna, a woodsman can gather in the spring and summer, guide in the fall, and hunt and trap in the winter. These activities are performances of the skill of woodsmanship, an intricate knowledge of the environment and the ability to maneuver in it.

The skills of woodsmanship are developed from an early age, and they serve as markers on the road to manhood. Trapper Tom Brown, who harvests from both woodlands and wetlands, recalls first learning to trap rabbits with handmade snoods, snares, and deadfalls when he was 11. He received his first knife the next year, on his twelfth birthday.

Family members are often important teachers, and the development of camaraderie is as important as the acquisition of skills. Recalls Brown:

> The ones that are killed, that's it, but the ones that are missed, that's the ones you really had the fun over 'em. I was with my grandson when— well, both of 'em—when they killed their first rabbit. But Bucky, when he got his first trout I was with him. When he got his first rabbit, when he got his first deer. So I told him week after he got his grouse—I was tendin' traps out at Coleman—so I said "Buck, there's another grouse out there." I said, "You go with me on Saturday morning. You'll be out of school. You'll get a crack at it." So we walked down the road, and lo and behold! The grouse kicks up. It went so fast he didn't even get a shot at it. I said, "Well, you got another chance, Buck." So we go around, and we get him in another open spot, and he missed him again! I said, "Buck,

did you hear what that grouse said when he took off?" He said, "No, but I'm gonna hear it." I said, "Well, I heard what it said. It said 'Bucky, you mighta killed my mate before but you couldn't hit my rear end with a barn door!'"[49]

Pelts and game meat have always been an important commodity in the Pinelands, especially for those who work the cycle. Although beaver, otter, mink, and skunk were trapped in the past, now they either require a special permit or are considered unmarketable. Fox, raccoon, and muskrat are still important quarry.

The woodsman's keen knowledge of the environment is his first tool for successful hunting and trapping. He knows both the habits and the routes of his prey, and that knowledge shapes his technique. One of the first tenets a trapper learns, in Tom Brown's words, is to "set down a great attraction and remove all suspicion."[50] Brown has a variety of methods for doing so, including dyeing traps in a walnut bath and removing human scent with red-cedar shavings. This removes suspicion. Among the tricks to create attraction is the use of liquid lures. Such potions as skunk essence, claims Brown, are responsible for the saying "Old trappers never die, they just smell that way." Finally, the trapper tries to create "eye appeal" by putting feathers, eggshells, or a piece of dry fur by the set to catch the attention of the prey.[51]

Brown formerly sold his pelts directly to Sears, Roebuck, and Company; today, trappers sell directly to fur buyers or to one of the large fur auctions.

The woodsman's ability to maneuver in the environment opens another occupational avenue to him: gathering. A vast array of plants grow in both dry uplands and wet lowlands of the Pinelands. Everywhere there is something worth collecting: pine cones in the Plains, Indian grass in the cranberry bogs, acorn sprays in the pitch pine lowlands, cattails and statice in the salt marshes, grapevines in the woods, bayberry at the seashore, sweetgum balls in domestic yards, sphagnum moss in the swamps, "cornettes" in corn fields, and a wide variety of huckleberries and blueberries in many places.[52]

Foragers know the worth of plants that are "just weeds" to other people. Farmers are often grateful to Leo and Hazel Landy when they ask permission to pick the podded mustard plant that clutters vegetable fields, or the okra that has gotten too woody to sell. To the Landys, the woodier the better.

Gathering has been an important part of the Pinelands economy for generations. Berger and Sinton point out that Americans have decorated their homes with dried and fresh flowers since Colonial times, and that the proximity of the Pines to major cities has provided a constant market. The fact that residents were supplying those markets abundantly as early as 1916 is underscored by botanist John Harshberger's worry that those who made bouquets and wreaths from Pinelands flora and sold them in Philadelphia were going to exhaust the supply of mistletoe, water lily, sweet-bay, holly, pink azalea, mountain laurel, and arbutus.[53]

In addition to the ready supply of plants, the independent lifestyle favored by residents has made foraging a widespread and well-favored industry. The variety of plants and plant life cycles offer a variety of occupational options to the woodsman. He can choose to concentrate on gathering certain plants from May through December, piecing the work year together with trapping or lumbering during the winter. He can gather occasionally to plug up smaller gaps in a work year that concentrates on hunting, trapping, and fishing. He can "moonlight" at gathering to supplement the income of a full-time job in business or industry. Or, like the Landys, he can rely on gathering, processing, and marketing to wholesalers for his entire subsistence.

Though well-equipped with his knowledge of plant types and cycles, the gatherer must still be willling to "get mud up to your eyebrows," according to Leo Landy.[54] His point might be broadened to mean that many plants are found in hard-to-reach places, and, further, that a gatherer must be prepared for a host of other inconveniences.

He must, first of all, be willing to let nature set his alarm clock. Many plants are marketable only at a certain stage of growth, and a good woodsman will recognize that often brief period and time his work schedule to it. If dock (*Rumex crispus*), for example, is picked when it's too green, it will turn a dull brown instead of the bright russet color that florists prefer. On the other hand, if it is "too far gone," it will shed its seeds and lose its shape.[55]

Various plants get specialized handling in order to bring out their best colors and textures. For instance, the Landys gather the dark brown pod of sensitive fern in low spots in the woods after first frost. They cut them with a sickle, leaving a 14-inch stem, tie them loosely in bunches, and place them, pod end up, in baskets to dry. Because the pods will lose color if they are dried in high temperatures such as those in a hothouse, they set them in a storehouse for three to four days. Only after they are fully dry are they boxed for sale.

For many people, the pine cone is a natural symbol of the region. Its importance to gatherers makes this especially appropriate. Though sales usually fluctuate from year to year, the Landys may process and sell as many as 70,000 pine cones in a year.[56]

Although both Virginia pine and pitch pine grow in the region, most gatherers prefer to pick the cones of dwarf pitch pines because the trees are shorter. They are also thickly covered with cones that produce a lot of seed, an important trait to processors who sell the seed as well as the cones.

A woodsman will recognize the age of a cone by its color: this year's crop is green; last year's is grayish-brown; and the previous year's is grayish-black. Although second-year cones are saleable to dealers who paint cones, the green cones are preferable. They are still tightly closed and will open into a shiny brown rosette when heated in a "pine cone popper." Third-year cones are often wormy and therefore disintegrate in the heat.

Bill Wasiowich gathering pine cones. Photograph by Joseph Czarnecki. PFP219558–9–12A.

A gatherer times his harvest for both ease and conservation. "You wait till frost," says Jack Cervetto. "The cone is mature then and it's kinda dryin' up and it snaps off the vine easier. You go to pull that off [out of season], that's so sticky with pitch now you have to get half the branch with it. Do an awful lot of damage to the tree, lettin' that sap right out of it. Then for about five years you won't get any more pine cones out of that tree. You got the best nourishment out of it."[57] Moreover, woodsman Bill Wasiowich observes that trees produce cones more abundantly when they are picked regularly.[58]

Although today most gatherers sell their cones to processors such as Landy, the "pine cone popper," a crude brick or cement building with a tin roof, is common to the Pinelands because many woodsmen at one time or another gathered and processed cones. The "popper" acts as a giant oven in which to heat cones with slow, wood-fired heat; this dries and opens them.

In addition to their commercial value, forage plants have personal value for Pinelands residents who use them as a medium for aesthetic expression in traditional forms such as wreaths, bouquets, and grave blankets. The grave blanket is a highly localized form, according to folklorist Susan Samuelson. It is especially popular in the southern agricultural area of the Reserve. While it has become an important commercial item for produce merchants, it continues to be what it began as: a traditional Christmas decoration created by families for their burial plots.

Generally, a grave blanket is constructed on a base of wood and sphagnum moss. Evergreen boughs such as spruce or scotch broom are arrayed on the base to form a flat spray. The size varies, but two feet by three feet is standard. Decorations of either natural materials, such as pine cones, laurel, or red ruskus, or artificial materials, such as ribbon and plastic ornaments, are usually added.[59] The blanket is placed on the grave around the first Sunday in December.

Although there are analogues in other places, the grave blanket in southern New Jersey most clearly expresses the close association of human society and natural environment. Hazel Landy recalls that her father would always add a few pieces of princess pine to the blankets he made. Now, she says, she always does the same on the blankets she makes for the family plot.[60]

Probably more pervasive, but less well documented, has been the use of Pinelands flora in foodways and in folk medicine. Poke, for instance, has traditionally been gathered in spring and cooked like tender greens. Wild huckleberries, blueberries, and cranberries have been gathered for pies and jellies.

Portrait of James Still, the "Doctor of the Pines," Medford, New Jersey, circa 1877. From Early Recollections and Life of Dr. James Still, Philadelphia: J. B. Lippincott, 1877.

His use of gathered ingredients was part of the reason for the fame of Dr. James Still, the son of two slaves from Maryland who bought their freedom and settled in South Jersey. He was born in 1812 at Indian Mills in Burlington County. His brother, William, was active in the abolitionist movement and was the author of a book about the Underground Railway.

Still was not formally trained in medicine, but learned about medicine by observing druggists on visits to Philadelphia and by reading books on botany. He adapted this knowledge to the woodland environment around him when he moved in 1827 to Medford and began practicing folk medicine. Other physicians in the area disapproved of his practice, but many people in the Pines near Medford attested to the effectiveness of his cures. In 1877, he published an autobiography entitled *Early Recollections and Life of Dr. James Still*. The following recipe used some of the plants he gathered in the western fringes of the Reserve at Medford:

Take

Spikenard root	8 oz.
Comfrey root	8 oz.
Horehound tops	8 oz.
Elecampane root	8 oz.
Bloodroot	8 oz.
Skunk-cabbage root	8 oz.
Pleurisy root	8 oz.

All bruised; then boil in two gallons of soft water down to one gallon; express and strain the liquid, and see that you have one gallon. Then add ten pounds of white sugar, and boil to form a syrup. When done, strain again into something to cool, and when nearly cool take two drachms oil anise and four ounces alcohol, mix and pour into the balsam; also one pint tincture of lobelia. Let the whole stand twenty-four hours to settle, then bottle up in half-pint bottles. Dose:—One teaspoon three, or five times a day. This balsam far excels anything I have ever known used for pulmonary affections and coughs of long standing. It is admirably calculated to relieve that constricted state of the lungs which is so often met with in consumption. It assists expectoration and invigorates the whole system, and is seldom or never given without benefit. This is an excellent remedy for asthma or any bronchial affection attended with difficulty of respiration.[61]

Lake Communities and Ethnic Resorts

Since the nineteenth century, there have been various attempts to develop resorts, retirement communities and suburbs in the Pinelands. Some of these schemes, like the plan of a Long Island real estate promoter to develop the "Magic City" of Paisley between 1888 and 1891, came to naught.[62] Other plans, such as the development by Gloucester Farm and Town Association of Egg Harbor City and its vicinity as an agricultural center, were very successful. Many of these land developments, which centered on the adaptation of old millponds and former cranberry bogs to new uses as recreation centers, grew with the change in attitudes toward wilderness.

The history of Lakewood traces such an evolution. Its first use was as the site for the Three Partners' sawmill, erected circa 1786, on a branch of the Metedeconk River. The mill was replaced first by the Washington Furnace, which was in operation between 1814 and 1832, and then by the Bergen Iron Works, which operated there between 1833 and 1854. Joseph W. Brick was the proprietor of the latter until his death in 1847. In 1865 the place was named Bricksburgh, and in 1866 a company named Bricksburgh Land and Improvement Company was formed to develop the land into fruit farms. In 1879 the company sold its interests to a land association that renamed the place "Lakewood" and attempted to develop a winter resort there. Apparently the effort was successful, for in 1889 Gustave Kobbé described Lakewood in the following words:

> *Lakewood* is a little winter paradise created by good taste and sound judgement backed by the necessary capital, on the site of one of the iron furnaces which formerly reared their stacks among the pines. . . . There are few places which one recalls with as much affection as Lakewood. It has the tranquility of a refined home while affording a varied range of amusements. Though a health resort, it is not over-run with invalids, so that a person who goes there for relaxation does not have his spirits dampened by silent but no less piteous appeals to sympathy. In fact, Lakewood is a place of rest rather than a health resort. People go there to recuperate after a rapid social season or to tone up the nerves after they have been subjected to an unusual strain.[63]

The site was laid out around Lake Carasaljo, which was named after the three daughters of Joseph W. Brick—Caroline, Sarah, and Josephine. Scenic roads intended for driving, riding, cycling, and walking wound through the woods around the lake, and the Laurel House Hotel graced the town. Kobbé described the hotel in glowing terms:

> The Laurel House is old-fashioned in that it is home-like; and modern in that it lacks none of the latest improvements. Among its sources of comfort are the ample hearth in the sitting hall . . . ; its parlors and reading room; its spacious and well-equipped nursery; a smoking room in which whist, a game as aristocratic as the gout, is assiduously cultivated; its *cuisine,* admirable and abundant; its piazzas of 380 feet, which are glassed over and kept at an agreeably warm temperature so as to form a pleasant promenade in wet weather; and the open fireplace in all the bedrooms, wood fires being supplied free of charge. There is also a large hall for music and dancing.[64]

In the twentieth century, Lakewood became a Jewish winter resort, perhaps because of its proximity to the Jewish poultry farmers in Farmingdale. Today a number of ethnic groups have settled there, including Orthodox and Hasidic Jews, and Estonians.

Medford Lakes grew from similar roots, but in a different direction. On the tributaries of the Upper Rancocas Creek, it, too, began as the site of a sawmill. In 1766, Charles Read established Etna Furnace in the vicinity. By 1770, there was a small stamping mill, a gristmill, and a furnace on the site. Read also built the furnaces at Taunton, Atsion, and Batsto. But he experienced both health and financial difficulties in the early 1770s, and he moved first to Antigua and then to St. Croix. His son, Charles Read, Jr., inherited Etna Furnace in 1773, but with his death in 1784, the land passed out of the hands of the Read family. Under the new owners, who renamed it Etna Mills, the two sawmills and the gristmill continued. Some cranberry cultivation was tried, too, but it was unsuccessful. Finally, in 1927, a Texas land speculator named Captain Clyde W. Barbour bought the property with the idea of developing a summer colony around the 21 lakes or potential lake sites it encompasses. Barbour's representative was a real-estate man named Leon Edgar Todd, who eventually bought out Barbour's interests. Todd moved to Medford Lakes, as it was renamed, and supervised the laying out of roads, trails, lakes, beaches, parks, and building lots.[65] The houses were built in a log-cabin style, a practice that persists today. In 1928 a community house named "The Pavilion" was constructed, and in 1930 the Medford Lakes Lodge, said to be the largest log-cabin hotel in the United States, was built. Soon the town was transformed from a summer resort to a year-round community of permanent residents.

Today residents belong to the Colony Club, which oversees care of the lakes and recreation facilities and activities in the borough.

Many of the permanent residents of Medford Lakes first used the area as a summer retreat. For them, the lake community offers the chance to maintain both a sense of personal isolation from city hubbub and the security of a readily available social network.[66] The lake becomes the focal point of community interaction as neighbors participate in the care, management, and surveillance of the lake. They also share special social events, perhaps best represented by the annual "canoe carnival" held every August.

The canoe carnival has been held for more than 50 years. Individuals, families, neighbors, and members of organizations who live in Medford Lakes compete with each other in the construction of large and brilliantly lit floats that are supported by canoes. Each entry may use no more than two canoes and two paddlers. The challenge is in moving the canoe, with its elaborate assemblage, around Lake Aetna without capsizing.

Power boats are not allowed on the lakes in Medford Lakes for ecological reasons. However, along with the "Indian trail" names that mark the streets, and the rustic architectural style of the homes, the use of canoes is a conscious attempt to link the modern community with a mythical past.

In Cassville, in the northwestern reaches of the Pinelands, a golden onion dome gleams incongruously among the green pine tops. It crowns St. Vladimir's Russian Orthodox Church, one of the two churches that serve and symbolize the Russian community of Rova Farms. The Pines offered to this group both a healthful resort area and a rich supply of environmental features which could support ethnic folklife.

In 1926, Russians who had migrated in the late nineteenth and early twentieth centuries to big cities in New York, New Jersey, and Pennsylvania, founded the Russian Consolidated Mutual Aid Society to provide support and assistance to each other in times of need. One perceived need was to get people out of the crowded cities and into the healthful countryside, so in 1934, the association, by then known as ROOVA, bought 1600 acres of land, including a mill lake, just north of Lakewood. It was then resold in smaller plots to ROOVA members for vacation and retirement homes. Eventually a community center, restaurant, gift shops, cemetery, home for the aged, and churches were built. Many families settled there permanently.

At Rova, the residents have used the natural resources of the Pinelands to re-create old world ambience. Birch trees, a prominent feature of both Eastern European and Pinelands forests, have been annexed literally and figuratively into the landscape of this Russian community. A row of birches flanks

Following overleaf:
Blessing of the water,
St. Vladimir's Day
Russian festival at
Rova Lake in Cass-
ville. Photograph by
Dennis McDonald.
New Jersey State Coun-
cil on the Arts.

the walkway to the center, and small trees and branches are often used for decoration on holy days such as Pentecost and at community festivities.

During the celebration of St. Vladimir's Day in July, ceremonies commemorate the Christianization of Russia by St. Vladimir. The blessing of the waters is a traditional element of the day, and at Rova, the ritual takes place beside the lake.

Another important resource that the Pinelands offers the Russian community is the panoply of mushrooms that grows there. Mushrooms are an important ingredient in Russian cooking. After being dried or pickled, they appear in many dishes, especially during the meatless Orthodox Lenten season. Mushroom hunting is a skill that Russian girls learn from their mothers. Pinelands forests offer a wide variety of microenvironments to nurture the different "communities" of mushrooms that women such as Dusia Tserbotarew and Valia Petrenko have learned to recognize in particular places such as under nut trees and on old stumps.[67]

Two other Russian communities have made their homes in the Pinelands. After the Russian Revolution, a number of Byelorussians who had been officers in the Tsarist army migrated to New York City. In the 1940s some of them moved to Lakewood Township to engage in chicken farming. A third group of Russians came to America as displaced persons after World War II. This wave included a group of Kalmyks, Mongolian Buddhists who had migrated to southwestern Russia in the sixteenth century. They were temporarily housed in barracks in Vineland, and some of them later settled in Freewood Acres north of Lakewood.

Cedar miner holding a "progue," 1937. Courtesy of George H. Pierson, New Jersey Bureau of Forest Management, Division of Parks and Forestry.

SWAMPS

Cedar Shingle Mining

Over the years, Pinelands swamps have offered exotic products to woodsmen resourceful enough to find uses for them. Surely one of the most unusual was Atlantic white cedar that had been buried in the rich muck for centuries. In the eighteenth century, it was discovered that thousands of these logs lay deep in the swamps of Dennisville. Until the early twentieth century, they were excavated, or "mined," from the swamps and used, because of their preserved state, to make shingles. Thus the men who mined cedar were known as "shingle miners."

Raising, or mining, cedar timber, circa 1857. From Geological Survey of the County of Cape May. Trenton: The True American, *1857.*

The shingle miner first probed the muck with an iron rod, known as a "progue," to locate the cedar log. Then he dug into the tangle of roots with a "cutting spade" and sawed off a section about one foot long, called a "cut-off," which would pop to the surface like a cork. If he determined that the log was of good quality, the miner then cut away the roots and dug out the muck, exposing a hole that quickly filled with water. He sawed off the ends and, using levels, raised the log. When free, the log floated to the surface and turned over.

The shingle miner used a crosscut saw to cut the log into shingle lengths. Then he used a mallet and froe to split it into blocks called "bolts." Each bolt was then split into shingles. The rough shingles were dried in the sun and then shaved with a drawing knife on a shaving horse.[68]

Charles Pitman Robart was the last shingle miner in Cape May County. He was born at Dennisville in 1828, and he died there on September 29, 1907, in his seventy-ninth year. Edwin Robart, his son, wrote the following reminiscences about his father and shingle mining in a letter quoted by Charles Tomlin in 1913:

My experience with my father in removing these logs from the soil and converting them into shingles was, from the time I arrived at the age of

Sawing cedar logs and making shingles. From Geological Survey of the County of Cape May. *Trenton: The True American, 1857.*

ten until I was sixteen years of age, always in the summer when I was out of school.

. . . No doubt the greatest place where these logs were found was in what is known as Robbin's Swamp. This swamp was cut off about 1864, enabling miners to investigate the bottom. The result was that hundreds of thousands of these shingles were taken out as there were several shingle miners at the time. Roads had been made of poles and bark to get the live timber out, and these same roads were used to cart out these shingles. Shingles secured in most places had to be carried out on the backs of men and boys to the creek and then taken by boat to the landing.

. . . Father secured thousands of these shingles in what is known as Hawk Swamp. . . . I being a boy could carry but twelve of these shingles if they were shaven as soon as they were dug, which was quite frequently the case. If the shingles could be dug and allowed to dry thoroughly, a man could make much more headway in shaving them. Father was considered a fast worker and could shave six hundred a day. With things favorable, he could mine and get ready for market one thousand shingles per week which usually sold for $16. In later years when sawed shingles came on the market, the price was as low as $12, which was very poor pay for mined shingles.

. . . For a number of years after the Civil War, in which he served, father was engaged in the milling of grain, but after the mill blew out he returned to shingle mining, following it until he was 76 years of age.[69]

Pinelands residents continue to be fascinated by the phenomenon of mined cedar and its products. Charles Pomlear recalls logs that were dug up when he worked at the Durell plantation: "I could show you cedar trees in there that you and I, if they were standing, couldn't reach around them, three or four of us."[70] They conjecture about how the smell of the cedar chip conveyed information, suggesting that a windfall would contain sap. Cedar shingles, and homes that still wear them, are valued pieces of local history. One man, it is said, has refashioned them into cabinets for his home.

Cedar Farming

"That's our wood, Tom," was Ed Hazelton's response to folklorist Tom Carroll's query about why he uses Jersey white cedar for his miniature boats.[71]

Indeed, the tree and its wood have been distinctively a part of both the economy and the identity of the Pinelands throughout its history. Cedar's lightness and durability have made it a favorite for export and for regional uses. In 1749, traveler Peter Kalm described it:

A tree which grows in the swamps here, and in other parts of America, goes by the name of the white juniper tree. Its trunk indeed looks like one of our tall, straight juniper trees in Sweden: but the leaves are different, and the wood is white. The English call it white cedar, because the boards which are made of the wood, are like those made of cedar. But neither of these names is correct, for the tree is of the cypress variety. It always grows in wet ground or swamps; it is, therefore, difficult to get to it, because the ground between the hillocks is full of water. The trees stand both on the hillocks and in the water: they grow very close together, and have straight, thick and tall trunks; but their numbers have been greatly reduced. In places where they are left to grow up, they grow as tall and as thick as the tallest fir trees. They preserve their green leaves both in winter and summer; the tall ones have no branches on the lower part of the trunk.[72]

More recently, boatbuilder Joe Reid called it ". . . the best wood that grows for boats," and described its virtues for boatbuilding. It planes well, doesn't split off, and has a long grain that can be steamed and shaped to the forms of Jersey boats.[73]

Cedar grows crowded together in small scattered stands throughout the Pinelands, taking from 80 to 100 years to mature. Although the crowding slows down its growth, it enhances its survival. Cedar trees are easily toppled by the wind, and Pinelands cedar farmers have classified the types of wood produced by "windthrow." "Boxy" cedar is the dense wood produced when a thrown tree eventually rights itself. "Shook" timber has inner cracks caused by twisting of the tree in the wind.[74] "Brazile" or "brasilie" is the exceptionally hard wood formed by cedar that has been in too much water. Oldtimers would detect it by putting a suspect board in the sun; it would quickly curve up if it were brasilie.[75] "Brassy" cedar is full of knots from the low branches that grow after the top of a cedar tree is burned.[76]

Many cedar farming methods aim to produce "clear" cedar that is free from knots. Adequate crowding inhibits the formation of branches, which cause knots. But all seedlings and saplings will not survive, so cedar farmers wisely thin the crop of marketable poles.

The uses of cedar have been many and varied over time. Kalm catalogued some of them:

> The white cedar is one of the trees which resists decay most; and when it is put above ground, it will last longer than underground. Therefore it is employed for many purposes; it makes good fence rails, and also posts which are to be put into the ground; but in this point, the red cedar is still preferable to the white. It likewise makes good canoes. The young trees are used for hoops, round barrels, turns, etc., because they are thin and pliable; the thick, tall trees afford timber and wood for cooper's work. Houses which are built of it surpass in duration those which are built of American oak.[77]

Today, Jersey white cedar fortifies both artifacts and traditions throughout the Pinelands. Boatbuilders make Jersey garveys and Barnegat Bay sneakboxes, and carvers shape decoys and boat models from it. Delaware Bay oyster schooners are kept alive with cedar planks, and coastal docks and bulkheads are kept afloat with cedar posts. Cedar clam stakes mark underwater beds in the bays, and cedar stales (long handles) move clam tongs onto those beds. Pole limas climb cedar poles in South Jersey gardens.

"You could use the regular two-by-twos from the lumber yard, but the cedar has a rough bark that makes it very easy for the beans to climb on," said George Heinrichs. "Yeah, like Jack and the beanstalk, if you had one twenty feet in the air, he'd go clear to the top of it."[78] Cedar trees are often used as Christmas trees, and many residents understand why Helen Zimmer ". . . couldn't live in a place where there's no Jersey white cedar," so thoroughly has the culture incorporated the wood into its existence.[79]

Although other methods of entering the swamps are used by most cedar farmers today, the building of "corduroy roads" to carry horses and wagons into the swamps was long an important activity. Pinelands swamps are replete with these paths, also known as "pole roads," "causeways," and "crossways." So important are they that they have names. One of the oldest, Frankie's crossway, dates back to the eighteenth century. One of the newest, Collins's crossway, was built by Clifford Frazee and his son, Steve, recently.

The Frazee family has lived in Forked River for generations, and the water in the area has always been vitally important to the family. Cliff's father oystered in the Barnegat Bay until the water became too saline in the 1930s. The oysters stopped growing in the bay, and Cliff turned to the

Cedar-lined Bible chest made by Cliff Frazee, Jr., and cedar cradle made by Steve Frazee. Lent by Cliff Frazee, Sr., and Steve Frazee. Photograph by Anthony Masso.

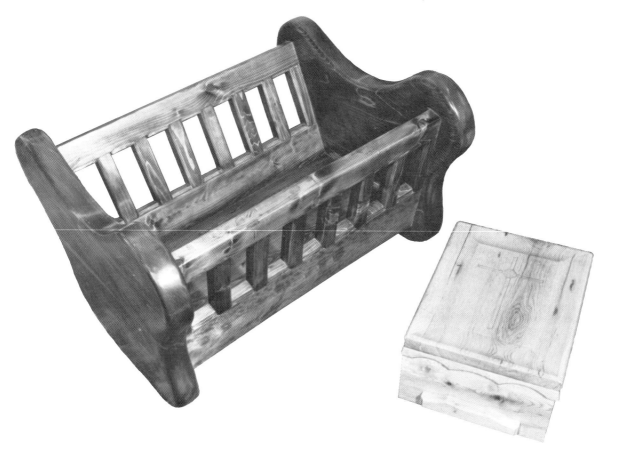

woods and swamps for his living. He worked a cycle that included scooping cranberries, clamming, cutting wood, and working for the state.

In the 1950s he started buying cedar swamps. Eventually, he bought a 600-acre tree farm and a mill, which Steve now runs. Since that time, wood, especially cedar, has been an integral part of both work and family.

Cliff's home grew with his family, acquiring cedar closets and bathroom, sassafras trim, and pine-paneled walls. In the living room, an oak Bible chest lined with cedar protects the family Bible, a two-century-old heirloom inscribed with the genealogy of the family. When the family inherited the book, Cliff, Jr., the eldest son, made the chest.

Steve Frazee lives nearby with his wife and four sons in a home that he built, principally from cedar. His esteem for wood is reflected in the many ways he finds to display its grain and color. Much of the furniture was also built by Steve, and some items seem particularly invested with a sense of family continuity. Before they married, Steve made a cedar hope chest for his wife. All of Steve's sons spent their first months in a cedar cradle he made, as well. "When I build things," says Steve, "I like to build them right. It takes a little longer, but I wanna build so it'll last forever. See, that's the way I think." [80] Individual trees prompt imaginative expressions of sense of place: "One tree I saw down right by Frankie's crossway. The tree was about this big. But when the tree was this big, they cut the surveying line across it. You could see, as I sawed it, I could see where they cut each branch off, a long time ago. And I took the one tree, and I was thinking about makin' a wall out of it, then this tree would be a history of when that surveying line was cut." [81]

Two days a week, most weeks of the year, the Frazees go into the swamps to cut cedar. During the dry season, they work each day on the crossway that carries them into the swamp and allows them to carry cedar out. To build a crossway, or corduroy road, they first mark the borders of the road, using a chain saw. They then level the roadbed by removing the stumps, first cutting horizontally along the bottom of the stump with a chain saw and then cutting vertically to the level of the horizontal cut. They discard the roots and compress the moss and dirt into the spongy ground. Next, they lay cedar, maple, and gum logs of less than four inches diameter horizontally along the road, with the thinnest logs in the middle and the thicker logs at the outer edges where the wheels of the truck will run. In order to level the road, they place a load of slabs from the mill between the logs already laid. Then they place more slabs perpendicular to the first level. Finally, they place on top trimmed limbs from cedar trees with the crotch ends facing outward and the brush ends facing inward. [82]

Cliff Frazee and his son, Steve, loading cedar logs on his truck. Photograph by Joseph Czarnecki. PFP215661– 2–8A.

Nature has much to say about how and when they work. The swamp is full of holes and soft spots that can practically swallow heavy equipment. The sawyer must maintain his balance as he cuts. Swamps that have not been burned for a long time become nearly impenetrable with undergrowth. Woodsman George Brewer facetiously named one particularly dense and dangerous area "Laurel City." Trees are felled toward the crossway, so cutting can only be done when the wind is blowing in the direction in which they want the trees to fall.

Cutting a tree takes about 30 seconds. Steve cuts and notches the tree and Cliff pushes it to fall into the clearing. Both men then trim the branches from the entire trunk with axes. They cut the logs into 16-foot lengths and drag them to the roadside where they will be picked up the next day and hauled out of the swamp.[83] The remaining days of the week, the Frazees mill the wood at the sawmill near Double Trouble.

In 1749, Peter Kalm fretted about the depletion of cedar.

Cliff Frazee of Forked River standing on a crossway. Photograph by Joseph Czarnecki. PFP216395– 6–34.

In many parts of New York province where the white cedar does not grow, the people, however, have their houses roofed with cedar shingles, which they get from other parts of New Jersey, to the town of New York, whence they are distributed throughout the province. A quantity of white cedar wood is likewise exported every year to the West Indies, for shingles, pipe staves, etc. Thus, the inhabitants here, are not only lessening the number of these trees, but are even extirpating them entirely. People are here (and in many other places) in regard to wood, bent only upon their own present advantage, utterly regardless of posterity. By these means many swamps are already quite destitute of cedars, having only young shoots left.[84]

Today Cliff Frazee worries, too, but, knowing that clear-cutting a swamp provides the best chance for regrowth of young seedlings, he worries more about the water—its depth, flow, and salinity. As long as there is sufficient moisture, cedar will regenerate and seedlings will thrive. With too much water, cedar saplings will drown. Although natural damming often maintains an adequate water level, Cliff believes that a good cedar management plan would allow damming to maintain depth. If the water does not become brackish, cedar will continue to grow in the Pinelands swamps, and future cedar farmers may one day mark Cliff Frazee's handiwork on an old corduroy road as they harvest a 70-year-old stand of cedar.

Moss Gathering

"There is no rug prettier, with its golden fringe around it," Jack Cervetto told ethnobotanist Eugene Hunn.[85] The rug Cervetto refers to is sphagnum moss. It carpets Pinelands swamps, where tall cedars crowd, their dark green tops a canopy over soggy depressions furnished with cedar hassocks and unusual plants. "Hassock" is the name that natives have given to the gnarled and knobby root systems of cedars that poke out of the water at the base of the tree.

Because swamps punctuate the woodlands, moss was for many years a staple in the gathering calendar of most woodsmen. Sterile and highly absorbent, it was used as a base for floral arrangements and in surgical dressings. In the 1950s, however, a shift in Pinelands' manpower to heavy industry and the invention of styrofoam simultaneously reduced supply

and demand. Today, a few gatherers still harvest and process the moss, including Bill Wasiowich of Woodmansie.

Wasiowich takes wheelbarrow, bucket, and pitchfork into swamps over
old crossways abandoned by cedar cutters. He "pulls" the moss, hauls it out
of the swamp, and takes it back to his homestead, where he spreads it on the
sandy ground. With rakes that he makes himself, Bill turns the moss until
it is dry. Then he bales it in a moss press, usually a homemade contraption.

Methods of processing are like moss presses: highly varied but achieving
the same end. Because wet moss is so heavy, Jack Cervetto used to drape it
over the cedar hassocks in the swamp. After two or three days, the moss,
which could weigh as much as 200 pounds wet, would dry to a mere
15 pounds. He then would haul it out and press it into two-foot bales.

Woodsmen in the Pinelands have long visited the swamps to harvest
moss and cedar, but for men such as Cervetto, the swamp offers greater
rewards: "I like other woods, yeah, the Plains. But if you get right in the

Jack Cervetto of Warren Grove. Photograph by Joseph Czarnecki. PFP222306–3.

middle of a cedar swamp with a good growth of cedar, you really think that you're the only person in the world. You're closed in there in a way that gives you the feeling there's nobody else around. And the smell! Yeah, I love that sphagnum smell. Boy, that's somethin'. I found out that's why I like workin' moss and cedar." [86]

MEADOWS

Salt Hay Farming

In 1879 the Reverend Allen H. Brown, a local historian, described the New Jersey meadows:

> The salt marshes or salt prairies of the coast may be reckoned among the natural privileges, as they produce annually, without cultivation, large crops of natural grasses. The arable land comes down to the sea in the northern portion of Monmouth County, and again at Cape May; but in the long interval the sea breaks upon a succession of low sandy beaches. Between these long narrow islands, and the mainland, which is commonly called "The Shore," are salt meadows extending for miles, yet broken and interrupted by bays and thoroughfares. More than 155,000 acres of salt marshes are distributed along the coast from Sandy Hook to the point of Cape May, including also the marshes on the Delaware Bay side of that county. As of old, so now, they furnish good natural pastures for cattle and sheep all the year round, and are highly esteemed by the farmers whose lands border on them, as they constitute also an unfailing source of hay for winter use and a surplus for exportation. [87]

Local people call these wetlands "meadows." Like the bogs and swamps, the saltwater meadows bear crops that resourceful natives have found many uses for. Chief among these is "salt hay," a type of cordgrass (*Spartina*) that, like its upland namesake, sweet hay, was considered useful in the keeping of livestock.

Salt hay actually comprises three plant species which grow on slightly different elevations and are harvested together. Salt hay farmers recognize their subtle differences as keenly as they do the one- or two-inch variations in meadow height. "Black grass" (*Juncus gerardi*), a rush, grows earlier than

Following overleaf: Charlie Weber harvesting salt hay with a team of horses, a South Jersey wagon, and a scow at Lower Bank, circa 1940. Photograph by William Augustine. Courtesy of the Donald A. Sinclair New Jersey Collection. Special Collections and Archives, Rutgers University Libraries.

Opposite: Bill Wasiowich gathering sphagnum moss. Photograph by Joseph Czarnecki. PFP219558–9–35A.

the others and on higher meadows. It must be cut by July or it will become oily and black. *Distichlis spicata,* which salt hay farmer George Campbell calls "rosemary," has a slightly hollow stem and grows straight up on slightly lower elevations. "Yellow salt" (*Spartina patens*) is the very fine grass that grows at still lower elevations. Campbell calls it "the real salt hay" because of its excellent qualities.[88]

Over the years, salt hay has been put to many uses, and residents enjoy competitively cataloging those uses. In the eighteenth and nineteenth centuries, many farmers grazed their cattle on the salt hay in the meadows and also baled it for winter feed and bedding. At Harrisville, in the 1840s, it was used to produce as much as a ton of wrapping paper and "butcher" paper a day.[89] Farmers favor it for mulching sweet potatoes and strawberries because it will not sprout in upland soil. Salt hay farmer George Campbell's father even sold it to banana boats in Philadelphia.

In the nineteenth and early twentieth centuries, the sturdy bulk of salt hay made it a favorite for packing material in nearby glasshouses, pottery plants, and brickyards. It once held down the shifting sands of dunes that had been disturbed by real-estate development.[90] Because it doesn't rot, it has also been used in sewers. In Port Norris, factories used to make it into rope used chiefly in the casting of iron pipe. Jack Carney, whose father ran such factories, still supplies a small market from a backyard building with two machines.

Much of the salt hay farmer's work is an attempt to maintain a balance or rhythm with natural forces. Salt water nourishes salt hay, but if tides wash the meadows too often, according to George Campbell, sedges grow. The farmer must maintain his dikes and adjust his floodgates to control tidal wash on his meadows. The growth of grasses provides a sturdy surface to the undulating meadow. If left too long undisturbed, it becomes "rotten marsh" that can mire machines. Harvest and burning must be timed to deter this. Even with its protective mat, the meadow can be treacherous terrain. Knowledge and equipment enable the farmer to keep his balance on it.

In the early nineteenth century, salt hay was mowed with scythes and piled on parallel poles that two men would carry to a stack or boat. Later, both oxen and horses were used to pull mowing machines and sometimes to power hay-balers.[91] Campbell recalls:

We mowed it with a horse, and then we took another horse and we raked it with the old dump rake. We'd rake it into windrows, and then you'd turn around and reverse and put in what we called "cocks." Then we come in with the horses again, with the old wooden "shovel" ones that, you've seen pictures of them, years ago. And we'd pitch it all on the wagons and bring it ashore and then we'd put it in big stacks, loose. Well, there we got pretty mechanized. We had a boom with a cable on it with an old Hettinger engine that we had forks on. We would lift it off of the wagons in big forkfuls, okay? And stack it, and then all winter we had old stationary balers. We'd pull along from bent to bent and bale it in the big old three-wire stationary bales. And back then we'd still used to sell quite a bit loose, also . . . and we started on what I call my Cabin Marsh. My father used to go down there and bring it up on scows and boat it up creeks and, you know, to get it ashore.[92]

Farmer Ed Gibson of Port Norris remembered that it was necessary to keep two teams of horses, for one would sometimes have to pull the other out.[93] To avoid this, draft animals were specially outfitted. Oxen wore special collars; horses wore "mudboots." These shoes worked like snowshoes, giving the horse a broader base on the soupy meadow surface. Such shoes were made of wood or leather, and had "uppers" which came up on the front and sides of the hoof. They were secured with heavy straps and buckles. Other types modified the iron shoe, adding side loops or a wider base to it.[94]

Removing the hay required pole roads or scows. Pole roads were constructed by laying large, heavy poles, called "deadmen," lengthwise as a solid base, and then placing smaller poles or planks crosswise atop them. The deadmen were often made of cedar because it could withstand moisture. A hay scow was a bargelike boat that was pushed with a 15-foot cedar pole.[95]

Salt-meadow horseshoe. Lent by the Ocean County Historical Society. Photograph by Anthony Masso.

Harvesting salt hay, 1943. New Jersey Department of Agriculture Collection, Archives and Records Management, New Jersey Department of State.

Today, upland haying equipment is adapted for use on the meadows with balloon tires, traction belts, sleds, and flotation rings. A tractor-pulled windrower, baler, and wagon cut, bale, and move the hay. Where once a salt hay operation required 10 or 12 men, it now takes only 3 or 4.

The main task in salt hay farming has always been water control. Salt water is necessary for salt hay. It provides nutrients as well as irrigation. Campbell floods his meadows for six to eight weeks in the spring to control weeds and to fertilize for summer growth, but usually keeps tides out with dikes the rest of the year. If the meadows become too dry, however, upland weeds crowd out the salt hay. A system of drainage ditches and sluice gates facilitates the control of water.

Harvesting is usually done from June to January. Some spots, however, can only be gotten into during a hard (but snowless) freeze or a dry summer. If a field is uncut for longer than two years, it will be burnt over to destroy dead vegetation and encourage new growth. Drainage ditches, which must be kept clear, are also burnt.

The principal difference in equipment and methods for the salt hay farmer today is not the absence of the draft horse, but the presence of a giant crane and backhoe. While changes in equipment are usually caused by developments in technology, this change was caused by nature. For all the

George Campbell, salt hay farmer. Photograph by Joseph Czarnecki. PFP222306–6–35.

Delaware Bay salt hay farmers, the storm of 1950 marked the end of an era. The storm destroyed the natural banks of the meadows and upset the natural rhythm that had governed salt hay farming for generations.

Before 1950, the farmer's main task was cleaning the ditches and adjusting the gates. Since then, however, his major task has been building and maintaining the artificial banks against a rising sea level. ". . . So we're having to hold more and more water out of the meadows with the banks and it's getting, the economics is getting to the point that we're not gonna be able to do it much longer. It's going fast. I just keep running from one hole to another now on my cranes," Campbell says.[96] To compound the problem, tides have been higher in recent years.

Indigenous combatants in Campbell's fight to maintain a balance are wetlands animals and plants. Since 1950, *Phragmites communis* has claimed more territory in the meadows. This tall, plumed reed, while desirable to gatherers for use in dried arrangements, can outcompete *Spartina* under certain conditions. Campbell tried killing it with herbicide for awhile, but concluded that, like the mosquito, *Phragmites* will adapt to any adversity. "When something did come back," he told folklorist Jens Lund, "the *Phragmites* come back before anything else."[97]

Muskrats and otters can destroy banks, the "marsh bunny" with its burrowing and the otter with its play. Ed Gibson says otters "play like kids," sliding down the muddy banks.[98] Trappers are usually a welcome form of pest control.

Other creatures serve as alarm systems. While perch are normally found in the drainage ditches on Gibson's meadows, a carp is a signal that there is a break in the dike. Carp, which normally enter the meadow only during spring flood, and migrate out after spawning, may enter the ditches from the bay in search of roots if there is a break in the dike.

Though he may be fighting a losing battle with the bay, Campbell views salt hay farming as "a way of life," one followed by his father and grandfather before him, that he will not easily let go.[99]

Pest Control

For George Campbell, "half the enjoyment of working outside is going down in the meadow and seein' the osprey and the eagle taking the fish."[100] With the fiddler crab and the mosquito, the deer and the snow goose, they are familiar co-habitants of his environment. Not all of them elicit such favorable responses from Campbell, but their presence is part of the place and their absence a sign that something is amiss. When the meadows were sprayed with DDT to control mosquitoes, the crabs, dragonflies, fish, and mussels disappeared, too. Their return is welcomed as a sign that balance is back, even if it does mean more mosquitoes.

Pinelands residents know which creatures control others. They use their knowledge of these relationships in indigenous systems of pest control. Box turtles are kept in basements as silent snail catchers. Skunks are allowed to rid gardens of bugs and mice. Perhaps the most widely celebrated set in the Pinelands is the mosquito and the purple martin. The Jersey swamp mosquito ". . . is still bitin' you when everything else is dead and gone," according to local experience.[101] It long ago became part of regional identity. In 1685, a newcomer wrote: "In the Marshes are small flies called Musketoes, which are troublesome to such people as are not used to them."[102]

Peter Kalm's description in 1748 was more graphic:

> The gnats, which are very troublesome at night here, are called mosquitoes. . . . In daytime or at night they come into the houses, and when the people have gone to bed they begin their disagreeable humming, approach nearer and nearer to the bed, and at last suck up so much blood that they can hardly fly away. When the weather has been cool for some days the mosquitoes disappear; but when it changes again, and especially after a rain, they gather frequently in such quantities about the homes that their numbers are legion. The chimneys of the English, which have no dampers for shutting them up, afford the gnats a free entrance into the houses. On sultry evenings they accompany the cattle in great swarms from the woods to the houses or to town, and when they are driven before the houses, the gnats fly in wherever they can. In the greatest heat of summer, they are so numerous in some places that the air seems to be full of them, especially near swamps and stagnant waters, such as the river Morris [Maurice] in New Jersey. The inhabitants therefore make a fire before their homes to expel these disagreeable guests by smoke.[103]

Later, perhaps as proof of the power of humor to help people accept the inevitable, jingles, tales, and jokes featured the Jersey mosquito.

Kalm mentions one of the many methods of mosquito control that have been tried over the years—smoking. Another, suggested by a local newspaper, involved hanging over one's bed a rag that had been soaked in a mixture of camphor and whiskey.[104] Early in the twentieth century, the growth of tourism in shore areas prompted organized efforts at mosquito control.

These included glossing breeding grounds with kerosene, and eventually ditching and draining thousands of acres of salt meadow. These ditches, unfortunately, also contributed to the loss of many salt hay meadows. The spraying of DDT in the 1950s killed more mosquitoes but sterilized the meadows of other wildlife, as well.

While Pinelands residents are acquainted with a variety of natural enemies of the mosquito (including the scents of sphagnum moss and cedar), the traditional favorite is the purple martin, an insect-eating bird that summers in New Jersey. Long ago, the Lenape Indians, it is believed, removed most of the branches from tall saplings and hung gourds in them as homes for the martins. For over a century now, the square, gable-roofed martin house set atop a tall pole has been a familiar part of the landscape, especially in the open spaces near meadows, bogs, and blueberry farms. The martins' helpfulness with the mosquito problem, as well as their interesting habits, have earned them special status. This is reflected in the way people speak about the martin. In stories, it gains personhood and human characteristics: "They're your friend," says Leslie Christofferson. "In other words you can go out there, and when you'd shoot a starling, well, they'd be tickled to death. Oh, they'd whistle and talk to you. That's right! They knew you were helping 'em, believe it or not."[105] Starlings are a serious enemy of the martin, usurping nest compartments and sometimes even stealing eggs.

Christofferson, who lived most of his life in Whiting, New Jersey, has built many martin houses in his years as a carpenter and blueberry farmer. His observations of this species' social nature over the years prompted him to build a "purple martin palace." This masterpiece is more than six feet high and two feet in diameter, and weighs about 500 pounds. Though the structure adheres to the specifications requisite for a martin house, it elaborates on them in grand fashion. Each of its 112 apartments is reached through a hole that is about one and seven-eighths inches wide and has an inner dimension of approximately seven inches by six inches to give the bird space to build a nest and to turn around. "Just what makes common sense to you, you know, when you look at the bird."[106]

But more subtle aspects of the martins' social nature are catered to, with individual verandas on the eight-storied skyscraper:

You'd be surprised what personality they've got! And you'd have the same ones year after year on the same date. I could look out April the fifteenth, and I wouldn't see a bird. Maybe I'd start looking the fourteenth—I mean there within two or three days. After a bit, you'd look out there and you'd see waaay up there, maybe one or two birds. Way up in the air. Then the next day, half a dozen. Next day, twenty-five would come in. See, they'd go back and give them the signal—all's clear. They'd bring their families with them. And you'd go out there in the evening. The males sit out on the porches on a hot night. They were never in the houses, you know. You'd got out there, say, when the moon was bright, . . . and they'd lean over and talk to you. Oh, beautiful songs they have![107]

The purple martin palace was crafted through Christofferson's delight in both the creatures and the process of creation. It began simply enough: "I said, 'I guess I'll build a birdhouse,'" but grew, ". . . as a little challenge. I could build just about anything. I was going to build a round one, you know, but it turned out fourteen-sided. Fourteen sides. I divided it up and it came out just about right." And it ended with satisfaction: "Well,

Opposite: *Purple
martin palace. Lent by
Leslie Christofferson.
Photograph by An-
thony Masso.*
when I stood there, I said, 'Well, that looks like that should be it!' I built it right. There wasn't a joint you could get a razor blade in. It was built to perfection." [108]

Wetland Trapping

The meadows that fringe the rivers and bays are a transitional zone where a tug of war between earth and water goes on. In many places, meadows have been pulled violently back into the water, as along the Campbell's bay-side property. In others, the change was more gradual. Many of the meadows along the Maurice River were once fertile farmlands whose banks were reinforced by huge floating mud machines. Eventually, the river reclaimed them.

The amount of rainfall also affects these wetlands. When rain is scarce, the saltwater creeps landward, causing critical changes in both fresh and salt water bodies. For example, as the salinity increases on Delaware Bay oyster beds, the oysters are less able to resist disease. As freshwater meadows along the Maurice River become brackish, the "wild rice" that attracts the sora railbird disappears, and so does the railbird.

Yet residents of the wetlands have successfully adapted to change, both normal and cataclysmic. They have structured their lives around the daily fluctuations of the tides as well as the changes of the seasons. They've even met and mastered the considerable challenges of harvesting the resources of the muddy marshes, the muskrat and the snapper. People in Cumberland County have coined a name that celebrates this skirmish between man and nature and seems to declare man the victor. While those who trap, fish, and probe for turtles in other places are usually called "proggers," around Mauricetown they are sometimes called "mudwallopers." Chief among a mudwalloper's skills is maneuvering through the muddy areas where muskrats and snapping turtles can be found.

Albert Reeves of Mauricetown and his eight brothers learned these skills from their father, "Gummy" Reeves (so named because of his ever-present gumboots). According to Reeves, each man must know well the meadow he's trapping, watch for soft spots, and proceed with caution: "You wouldn't go along haphazard. You wouldn't just go along head up and not looking. You'd just sort of skid along, sort of feel your way along, feelin' for how much the mud's givin'. You can tell the soft spots. There's some water standin' there. The level spots would usually be the softer spots. When you get in a soft spot, you're out of luck." [109]

The consistency of soft spots varies greatly, calling for a variety of manue-vers: "I've seen my brother actually get down and swim in it! Thick, like a real thick puddin', it's so soft. He leaned over and actually swam to the boat, it was so soft."[110]

"Blue mud," recognized by its bluish cast, is more troublesome. It is more solid and sticky, with a consistency Reeves compares to putty. "It's terrible! Once you get in, you can't get out. That's how I hurt my hip, in blue mud, trying to pull my leg out. I've had trouble with it ever since."[111]

One animal that makes such hazardous pursuit worthwhile is the musk-rat, or "marsh rabbit," a small furbearer that is as abundant and valuable now in South Jersey as it was in 1749 when Peter Kalm made the following observation.

The muskrats, so called by the English in this country on account of their scent, are pretty common in North America; they always live near the water, especially on the banks of lakes, rivers and brooks. On traveling to places where they are, you see the holes which they have dug in the ground just at the water's edge, or a little above its surface. In these holes they have their nests, and there they stay whenever they are not in the water in pursuit of food. . . . Their food is chiefly the mussels which lie at the bottom of lakes and rivers. You see a number of such shells near the entrance holes. I am told they likewise eat several kinds of roots and plants. . . . They make their nest in the dikes that are erected along the banks of the rivers to keep the water from the adjoining meadows; but they often do a great deal of damage by spoiling the dikes with digging and opening passages for the water to come into the meadows; whereas beavers stop up all the holes in a dike or bank. They make their nests of twigs and such things externally, and carry soft stuff into them for their young ones to lie upon. . . . As they damage the banks so considerably, the people are endeavoring to destroy them when they can find their nests. The skin is sold and this is an inducement to catch the animal. The skin of a muskrat formerly cost but threepence, but at present they bring from sixpence to ninepence in the market. The skins are chiefly used by hatters, who make hats of the hair, which are said to be nearly as good as beaver hats. The muskrats are commonly caught in traps, with apples as bait.[112]

Muskrat is an important "cash crop" to many part-time trappers as well as to men who work the cycle full time. Boys who go to high school and men who work in offices and factories alike draw income from the traps they set and empty in the early hours each day between December 1 and March 15.

Tom Brown taking a muskrat from a trap. Photograph by Dennis McDonald. PFP219500–03–24.

On state-owned as well as privately held brackish tidal meadows that muskrats prefer, trappers set and tend traps on "low water," marking them with a pole. An experienced trapper may also time his activity to the weather and the mating cycle, therefore starting later and stopping earlier than the legal dates. Animal pelts "prime up" in the colder weather of January and thus are worth more when sold. Conversely, damage to fur caused by the fighting that occurs between males during the mating season in March lowers a pelt's value.[113]

To find muskrats, trappers may look for the "three-cornered grass" that they favor, and observe the maxim that "every animal has its highways"; the muskrat's are called "runs." Traps are set in the run about 50 feet from a "lodge," the mound of sticks, grass, and mud that houses the animal. A careful trapper will not step in the run. "Step your foot in it or mux it up in some way, and as a rule, he'll go somewhere else. That's the art of trapping."[114]

Both law and logic require trappers to visit their traps daily. An animal left unattended for a longer time may be damaged or stolen.

Little of the crop is wasted. Animals are first "skinned out," with the meat being frozen, eaten, or sold fresh by the trapper. Muskrat meat is often likened to a cross between wild duck and rabbit, and is a popular dish in the region. In Hancock's Bridge, just outside the Reserve, the annual Muskrat Dinner is always sold out. Trappers who also farm often use waste parts such as blood and bone, as fertilizer.

But by far the most valuable part of the animal is the fur. Value is expressed in many ways. The year 1980 is remembered as a good season because brown pelts brought $9.25 each. But an even more meaningful measure is often recorded in a statement such as, "My dad paid my college tuition that year with what he made trapping 'rats."

Fleshing out furs is therefore an important skill, for unremoved bits of fat can turn a fur rancid. Knife or push-pin holes can mar it. Tom Brown has developed equipment and methods to do this job to his high standards. A skinning bench with a "fleshing beam" mounted on heavy sassafras stumps provides a sturdy work base. After the pelt has been thoroughly scraped, it is slipped inside-out over a "stretcher" and hung to dry. Stretchers used to be made of wood, but are now most often made of wire.

Another denizen of the Pinelands—one more grotesque and cantankerous than the muskrat—is the snapping turtle, which lurks on the bottoms of brackish and freshwater ponds and streams from April through October and hibernates in the mud the other half of the year. Though the season is unregulated, it is difficult to capture the creature in months other than May to July in the traps that are most commonly used now.

Two other methods, which are only occasionally used today, were popular in the past. Telltale air holes on muddy flats indicate the presence of a snapper. The trapper probes with a large snapper hook until he hits a shell, then hoists the turtle up. The other method is called the "choker set," in which wire is wrapped in a groove around the middle of a four-inch piece of quarter-inch wooden dowel. The trapper tucks the stick into a piece of salt eel, fastens the choker to a line, drops it into a pond, and ties the line to a bush or a stake on shore. After the snapper swallows the bait, the choker turns crosswise so that it cannot be disgorged, allowing the reptile to be caught alive.[115]

Today, snappers are most often trapped in fykes. A fyke is a cylinder approximately five feet long and two feet in diameter. When made of net, the cylinder is supported by three evenly spaced wooden hoops. One end of the cylinder is entered through a net funnel that leads to a bait box. The other end is closed. Until fairly recently, the body of the cylinder was made of hand-knit net. Today it is usually made of wire fencing.

Whether in a pond or on a tide-washed meadow, the fyke is set so that one end of it will always be above water, and the turtle will not drown. This

Exterior of Tom Brown's hunting and trapping lodge. Photograph by Joseph Czarnecki. PFP221130-4-4.

may require anchoring the trap with sturdy poles or floating it with plastic buoys. On tidal meadows, the fyke is set on high tide and returned to on the next high tide.

Though snappers can be easily enough coaxed into a fyke with rank meat or fish, they can be safely gotten out only with caution and subterfuge. Tom Brown "bridles" the turtle by getting it to bite on a stick, then pulling the head back and tying it.[116] Other trappers spin the turtle to disorient it.[117]

Once out of the fyke, the turtle can be held by the tail, but only with the top of his shell facing away from the trapper. A snapper can only bend its head backward. The unwary trapper who gets bitten by a snapping turtle will testify to the power of his jaws, as do the sayings about the turtle. Some people chop off the head and cut it in two to prevent the snapper from

Interior of Tom Brown's hunting and trapping lodge. Photograph by Joseph Czarnecki. PFP217721–14–3.

biting for the two days after its death during which it is reputed to be capable of biting.

Most turtles are sold live to restaurants that may serve snapper soup with sherry on the side. Those that are used locally more than likely are served at parties at which a big pot of snapper soup with hard-cooked eggs in a vegetable-laden broth is the focus of enjoyment.

Railbird Shooting

Kenneth Camp's narrative on the origin of the name "railbird" recalls a time when gunning the birds was a far easier task than the one guides now experience:

This was a dairy farm in here. They used to have the split rail fence. And
when the meadows went out the fences went underwater, see, and
started floating all over. And these rails would get on them and line up.
They'd shoot them right down the rail. Yeah. That was more or less years
ago, you'd market hunt them. Wouldn't be nothing to come out and
shoot a hundred shells.[118]

Wildfowl are seldom so cooperative, and his knowledge of their habits and
habitats is a guide's stock in trade.

Guiding gunners of the railbird was an important part of the yearly
round for families such as the Reeves, who combined it with trapping and
fishing. Ken Camp, his father, and his son work things slightly differently;
they farm much of the year and guide gunners in the fall. Ken is also employed by the state as a forest fire warden.

In September and October, the "wild rice" (*Zizania aquatica*), or "wild
oats," as locals sometimes call it, attracts flocks of the tiny sora rail to the
freshwater marshes along the Maurice River in their migration south. These

meadows have names that recall the farmers who farmed them when they were diked: Hampton's Meadow, Coxe's Meadow, the Boudelier Meadow.

The bird, in turn, attracts gunners who rely on local guides to push them through the meadows atop the double-ended skiffs specially built for the hunt. The railbird skiff has two platforms, the rear one for the "pusher," who propels the boat with a long pole. Its relatively flat bottom, shallow draft, and pointed ends allow it to cut through the grassy meadows where the birds hide. The gunner stands near the front platform, gun poised.

"You gotta have a double end boat," according to Camp:

It has to be pointed so that you can push it through the reeds. . . . You gotta have them wide enough to make them stable, and long enough. The balance. You can't have a round bottom boat. You can't have a flat bottom boat. You gotta have more or less an in between, and you got to have a bow to them. The railbird skiff, mostly—the old ones were all made out of cedar. Cedar planking on the bottom. We modernized them by taking that off and putting plywood and fiberglass in them in the last

Railbirding skiff and push poles. Photograph by Dennis McDonald. PFP235042-2-10.

twenty years. Any of them that's built today is mostly built out of plywood and fiberglass. But there's not too many of them being built.[119]

The guide and the gunner go out about an hour before high tide in search of the seven-inch bird. It is easier to flush the rail during high water because it has no stable surface underfoot. Therefore, the hunt ends as the tide recedes.

As he poles through the meadows, the guide shouts the location of a bird for the gunner. If the shot is successful, the guide then poles the boat to the spot and retrieves the bird.

For a pusher, four critical aspects of a hunt are summarized in Reeves' maxim about what a guide hopes for: "Big tide, small man, good shot, big tip."[120] A big tide is one which comes in high and stands for a long time. The added depth it brings not only makes it easier to push the boat, but also causes the birds to flush more easily, producing "good shot," or many birds for the gunner.

It is easy to understand why a "small man" makes an easier day for a pusher. Yet it goes beyond lightness of load. As Camp explained to folk-lorist Gerald Parsons: "If you get a heavy boat and it's balanced out with a gunner, you can push it just as easily as you can another boat. The balancing out is the main thing, getting them going."[121]

Many of the people who have come to the Maurice River to shoot rail-birds have been wealthy and prominent. Names such as Kean, Straw-bridge, and Pugh are common in Reeves's repertoire of railbirding tales. A camaraderie between Reeves and the visiting gunners often developed and resulted in the "big tip" that could happily conclude a hunt for the pusher.

The good pusher needs numerous skills and reliable equipment to garner that big tip. In addition to a stable skiff, he wants a pole with a smooth, lengthwise grain that won't snap under stress.[122] He uses the pole with a side-to-side motion, creating a windmill effect.

The push poles used to be made of cedar, "but we get lazy, you know, and we go buy bannister rails out of the lumberyard." The pole has three blades on the end that prevent it from sinking into the mud. "The trick to pushing one of these boats," says Camp, "is really experience. It takes you a few trips before you can get on to it. You use your leg to steer with, and [learn] where to place the pole in the back of the boat."[123]

Because "you can do more in a half an hour at the right time than you can in three hours at the wrong time," a pusher must be able to read tides and weather fluently.[124] He'll avoid "pogee" (apogee) tides that are "lazy": they don't come in very far and they don't go out very far.

The two most important qualities of a good pusher are visual acuity and

strength, which enable him to spot birds and to push quickly and smoothly. Reeves, who hired many a local man to push gunners in his boats, explains: "Sometimes you have a real good pusher, but he can't mark so good. Then some guy could mark better, but couldn't cover as much territory, couldn't get around as fast. But you get the two together is what you got to do to get what you call a top pusher."[125]

The ecology of the region has changed as salt grass replaces the wild rice, which needs fresh water. "The salt grass is moving up more every year," Camp says. "Everything below the [Mauricetown] bridge is all salt grass now. Years back—say twenty years ago, twenty-five years ago—they used to hunt below the bridge. But that's all gone."[126]

RIVERS AND BAYS

Shipping

In 1862, after the death of his father the previous year, Alonzo T. Bacon of Mauricetown shipped out on the schooner *Robbie W. Dillon* which was owned by Captain George S. Marts, a neighbor and friend of his father:

> The occupations open to a boy, in which no capital was necessary, in any of the towns or villages in southern New Jersey were oystering, seafaring, or farming. I chose the seafaring life as being one by which, with determination to put forth my very best efforts, success would be achieved, and more remunerative occupation obtained.[127]

Advancement was quick for the right kind of person. Before he was 21 years old, Alonzo Bacon was a mate on the schooner *Thomas G. Smith,* and by the age of 23 he was the master of this same vessel. During his career as a coastwise schooner captain, he sailed to Boston, Charleston, Savannah, Baltimore, New York, Philadelphia, and also to Maine, Newfoundland, Nova Scotia, Texas, Louisiana, Florida, and the West Indies. In 1897, he sold his vessel to Captain William Crawford and bought the ship chandlery in Bivalve.

Until the building of the railroads in the late nineteenth century, and even a bit after, the products of the Pinelands were shipped by water from various landings along the rivers and bays.

Somers Point was the official port of entry for the entire Great Egg Harbor District. Each landing had a wharfmaster who maintained the wharf and collected a fee from boats using the dock. Jeffries' (also known as Jeffer's) Landing, on the Great Egg Harbor River, was named after John Jeffrey, who became wharfmaster in 1819. The goods shipped from his wharf included lumber, cordwood, charcoal, iron from Weymouth Furnace, farm produce, and salt hay from the meadows around the bay.

Various timber products were also shipped from English Creek Landing. In the last half of the century, cordwood was shipped to Haverstraw, New York, for use in brick manufacturing, and cordwood was carried to Philadelphia in small sloops called "bay craft."

By the first decades of the twentieth century, the railroad had completely eclipsed the sailing vessel, and in 1915 the customs district was officially closed.[128]

Boatbuilding

The importance of boats, their building and use, to southern New Jersey commerce and society were well captured by a visitor to Tuckerton who wrote in *Watson's Annals* in 1823:

> Little Egg Harbor was once (in my grandfather's time, when he went there to trade) a place of great commerce and prosperity. The little river there used to be filled with masted vessels. It was a place rich in money. Farming was but little attended to. Hundreds of men were engaged in the swamps cutting cedar and pine boards. The forks of Egg Harbor was the place of chief prosperity. Many shipyards were there. Vessels were built and loaded out to the West Indies. New York and Eastern cities received their chief supplies of shingles, boards and iron from this place.[129]

A wide range of boats have come from South Jersey boatyards in the past two-and-a-half centuries. Great schooners, coasting vessels, sloops, and shallops were crafted for work in the bays and ocean, while garveys, bateaux, sharpies, sneakboxes, and skiffs were, and in some cases still are, constructed for tasks such as sturgeon fishing and railbirding in the bays, rivers, and meadows.

These boatyards drew on the resources of the Pinelands. Many of them lay along the network of rivers and creeks which empty into Great Egg Harbor and drain the southeastern section of the Pine Barrens. They included two shipyards at Bargaintown on Patcong Creek and the Israel Smith yard on English Creek. Below Mays Landing, at the head of navigation on the Great Egg Harbor River, there were shipyards at Kats Landing, Pennington Point, Huggs Hold, Junk House Wharf, and Coal Landing, among others.[130]

Shipbuilding was also an important activity on the Dennis Creek in northern Cape May County. Dennisville, located five miles up the creek, produced at least 50 vessels between 1849 and 1901. Twenty-three of them were three-masted schooners up to 150 feet long. They had to be launched sideways and kedged down the creek by hauling in lines secured to anchors. It took several tides for them to reach the bay.[131]

On the Maurice River in Cumberland County, schooners were built both for coastwise trade and for oystering on Delaware Bay. The Lee brothers, two ship carpenters from Egg Harbor, founded a shipyard at Leesburg in 1795. A three-masted schooner was built at the Banner and Champion Yard in Dorchester in the 1880s.[132]

A large workforce was necessary for the many steps involved in constructing a wooden schooner. Skilled craftsmen, such as ship carpenters, caulkers, blacksmiths, and sailmakers, were drawn from the local population. John DuBois, a retired boatbuilder and oysterman, recalls that, "When I was young, the only thing to do in our town was either to work in the shipyard or go on to the boats."

Though workers were often motivated in their work by payment of a share in the ship's worth, DuBois cites the equally important reward of pride of workmanship: "You start with a pile of flitch lumber with bark on it, but when you get done you started from something with bark on [it] and you wind up with something that's finished, and you're proud of. There's a lot of satisfaction in building a nice boat."[133]

In the building of a schooner, the dimensions of the boat were first drawn on the mold loft floor. A carved half-model of the hull, which could be separated into cross-sections, was used. The framing timbers were cut from these patterns in symmetrical pairs. The keel, the backbone of the boat, was assembled, and the sternpost hoisted into position. Then the frames were also hoisted into position and fastened with wooden pegs known as "treenails" (pronounced "trunnels"), which would swell once the boat was in the water. The planks were steamed, fitted, and nailed to the frame, strake by strake, and the seams between the planks were caulked (made watertight) with oakum (hemp) and pitch. Then the masts, booms, gaffs, mast hoops, halyards, sheets, and blocks were installed. Typically a sailing schooner had two masts. The sails consisted of a jib, a staysail, a foresail, a mainsail, and topsails.

The age of steam power and of iron ships constructed in urban shipyards brought an end to the wooden shipbuilding industry in remote places such

Ship caulker at the Delaware Bay Shipbuilding Company, Leesburg, circa 1928. Photograph by Graham Schofield. Courtesy of John DuBois and John T. Schofield.

as the Pinelands. In the 1920s, the last wooden schooner was built in the Dorchester Shipyard on the Maurice River.

Boatbuilding in smaller operations continues today along the coast, however. Fiberglass pleasure craft are manufactured in Egg Harbor City, for instance, and much of the work on wood and engines is done by members of old coastal families.[134]

More common still is the backyard boat shop where garveys and sneakboxes are constructed by boatbuilders and fishermen who make boats for their own use.

Folklorist Tom Carroll's observation about the garvey, that it "results from the conjunction of local resources and local conditions," applies as well to other indigenous boat types—the schooner, sneakbox, and railbird skiff.[135] Each of these has been shaped by the local environment in which it is used, the particular tasks for which it is created, and the locally available materials and craftsmen.

Joe Reid, who knows boats from the standpoints of both use and construction, speaks for many residents when he says that Jersey cedar is best for Jersey boats. It has a long grain and can be steamed. This is in contrast to the "southern" cedar that he once tried to use. He explains that, "Every night we'd steam a board up in the bow, and clamp it, and leave it overnight. Next morning it'd be broke right in two. We didn't know that until we started using it." Fiberglass, another frequently used material, doesn't handle as well in water as cedar does: "Cedar takes in just the right amount of water. When it's first put there, it tends to sit right on top of the water. In a couple of weeks it soaks up the right amount of water and settles down. Then it handles really well. You can't beat cedar for a boat." [136]

The garvey, sneakbox, and railbird skiff are all tailored to the shallow waters they ply. Barnegat Bay, where garveys are used for clamming, ranges in depth from two to twelve feet, and the flat-bottomed garvey can pass in less than three feet of water. Water depths in grassy meadows where railbird skiffs are pushed and sneakboxes secreted are sometimes as little as two feet; consequently, those boats also have very shallow drafts.

The waterman's need for steady footing on the water is answered in the design of several of these boats. The garvey and the much larger schooner have each been described by users as "a sturdy working platform." The Jersey schooner is wide for its length, and the garvey has become wider over the years. Such proportions provide greater stability as well as ample deck space for the shellfish that they carry. The rail skiff provides a raised platform at each end. Its proportions and weight must be finely balanced in order for the pusher to maintain his balance. Albert Reeves, who pushed hunters on dozens of rail skiffs in his years, recalled one boat that missed the mark: "It had too heavy a frame. And not the right kind of flare. It was top heavy. I don't know how the hell I ever stayed on it!" [137]

Though they are all shaped by traditional templates, no two boats are alike, builders say. For one thing, the boat is often the collaborative product of the customer and the builder. John DuBois, who worked on the schooners, recalls that even oystermen sometimes played "keep up with the Joneses" by ordering the same boat a bit longer, larger, or grander. Others would have the boat tailored to their own way of sailing and dredging. [138]

James Reid, who works with his father, emphasizes that a craftsman continues to learn as he works: "I can't think of a single boat that we've done in the last five years that we haven't thought of something that coulda been done a little different. Only thing, my father would agree and say that you never really stop learning how to do it until you die." [139]

Yet good design, and the craftsmanship to execute it, is elusive, according to Albert Reeves: "It's hard to explain. I took one of my boats I loved so well—the design of it and everything—I took it to an expert, and took it there so he could make a copy of it, see. But it wasn't like it! He had the damn boat right there, but it still wasn't like it! He didn't know his stuff!" [140]

Les Hunter, who lived in Haleyville and built Reeves's favorite railbird boat (which he eventually sold to Frank Astemborski), did know his stuff.

For some boatmen, change is a problem. ("Well, sometimes you can't make things better than they are," said Albert Reeves.) Yet a skilled crafts-man alters his product within acceptable limits to suit a changed market or technology. Even though a tonger needs straighter sides on his garvey, Reid will flare the sides of pleasure garveys to meet the aesthetics of his customer. His work garveys have gotten wider to increase the load capacity, and the bow has been raised so that the boat rides higher in the water.[141] In such matters, Reid's judgment is so well regarded that people bring their boats to his yard so they can work on them under his practiced eye.[142]

Boats have a strong significance in the bay areas because of the personal and economic dependence on them; they are closely tied to many aspects of human life cycles. A waterman always remembers his first boat, whether it was an old garvey pulled out of the mud or the first oysterboat in which he "went up the Bay."

A boat is often the site of learning to work as well as becoming an adult in the community. Most men along the Delaware Bay have worked both in the boatyards and on the boats. In the words of Belford Blackman, a former oysterman, a youth would begin learning "how to work and how to work the boats" in the middle deck, where he would cull and clean up.[143] On the other hand, achieving the role of captain represented maturity and man-hood in the work community. In the past, recalls Fenton Anderson, an oysterboat captain was called "the old man," and the crew were "the boys," no matter what their ages.[144]

Captain Louis Peterson's recollection of his grandfather underscores the importance of boats in men's lives: "If it could be done with a boat, he did it. If it couldn't be done with a boat, it wasn't worth doing."[145] It is a sad occa-sion, therefore, when a man ends his work on the water and sells his boat: "I sorta hated to let it go. It was part of my life and everything. It was my last boat that I ever owned."[146]

Men are identified with boats and vice versa. In young Captain Todd Reeves's words, "If the boat don't do nothin', people will think of you as you don't do nothin'."[147] This attitude is reflected in the fact that most of the Delaware Bay oysterboats bear family names. Stories often refer to a man and his boat interchangeably:

> Tarburton was the captain of this boat, and this boat meant more to him than any boat he'd ever had 'cause she was the nicest and the biggest boat. And the first day of the season, we had an awful blow up here. I think he was the only boat that worked. Tarburton was the only boat that worked with that boat, and he planted two loads of oysters with her over in the state of Delaware.[148]

Opposite: Model schooner Charles Stowman made by the crew at the Stowman Shipyard, 1929. Lent by Albertson Huber. Photograph by Dennis McDonald.

Miniature garvey The
Gladys *made by Joe
Reid. Lent by Joe
Reid. Photograph
by Anthony Masso.*

Because of this importance of boats, the schooner has been appropriated as a symbol. A sailing schooner rides on the door of the Port Norris fire truck. In many homes, half models and pictures of family boats hang beside those of family members. A fully equipped scale model of a Jersey dredgeboat (oysterboat) was built by the workers in the Stowman Shipyard in 1929 to represent them in a Vineland parade.

The miniatures made by men such as Joe Reid, therefore, are meticulous statements of both sense of place and sense of person. Reid has spent his life in Waretown using and building boats. Now in his seventies, he seems to know everything there is to know about the garvey. Joe knows the subtle variations that occur in boats even within a limited region. When he was a boy, he recalls, the garveys in Tuckerton were lower and narrower than those in Waretown, and in Barnegat they used sharpies, a special rowboat that one rarely sees now.[149]

When he builds a boat, Reid says, "what I like is to let the wood more or less shape itself. Not try to force it. Have a graceful curve. No flat places in it."[150] His respect for the wood and his knowledge of the place have been crafted into the model garveys that Reid has made in recent years. He builds them of the same materials and according to the same methods as the full size boats, planing the cedar down to proportionate thickness and whittling by hand some tiny pieces such as the water scoop that he included in one model of a working garvey.

Though Joe attributes his first model to no grander a motive than "foolin' around," his miniatures really are grand statements writ small. They encapsulate a lifetime of experience, knowledge, and concern.

Fishing

The rivers and bays have enriched folklife in numerous other ways over the years. Along the Maurice River, proggers who trap muddy meadows for snapping turtles in spring and summer have also worked the river and bay for livelihood by fishing, shellfishing, and bird hunting.

Many fishermen believe that different species of fish come and go in great natural cycles. That seems to be the case on the Maurice River. Earlier in the century, striped bass (locally called stripers and rockfish) were so abundant that fortunes were made fishing them. By the 1970s their numbers had dwindled considerably.[151] Today, commercial fishermen are restricted from catching them in nets.

Another fish formerly caught in the Maurice was the sturgeon. Its value was greatly enhanced by its roe. Albert Reeves likes to recall being "up to my elbows" in caviar. Local men would process the roe of sturgeon before selling it to caviar companies in New York. The sturgeon would first be bled through the tail to avoid polluting the roe. The roe was then rubbed through a wire mesh to remove the fat and put in a clean wooden bucket, where it was salted in proportions of one pound of salt to ten pounds of roe. After several days, the roe was drained overnight on netting. Much of the roe that Reeves processed was sold to Ferdinand Hansen, a caviar dealer from the Fulton Fish Market in New York City.

The delicacy inspired little enthusiasm among the Reeveses, however, who sometimes used it in eelpots. Pickled sturgeon, though, is recalled with much relish.[152]

Menhaden ("bunker"), a valuable and prolific fish that has numerous industrial uses, was abundant along the Jersey coast until the 1950s. The huge schools of menhaden were encircled in purse seines (bag-bottomed nets) that were then drawn up by two dozen men in two striker boats. Their movements were coordinated with traditional songs called menhaden chanties.[153] Today, menhaden are caught in gill nets in smaller numbers and sold as bait.

Pound nets, which were actually huge fish traps that were often staked on the shore, were most often used in the past. Today, this and other methods, such as the fencing of carp as they emerge from meadowland ditches, are illegal. Still other methods, such as hauling seine and drifting gill nets, have changed only in their materials.

Before the invention of synthetic textiles, most fish nets were hand knit of cotton or linen with a large, flat wooden "needle" during idle winter months. Fisherman Nerallen Hoffman of Dividing Creek recalls the chant "Row upon row, watch it grow" that accompanied knitting sessions (which might include whole families).[154] The care of such nets was equally time consuming. After each use, a linen net had to be dragged through a lime box and put on a pole to dry. The coast in those days was lined with cedar drying poles spiked with nails.[155]

Today the weakfish, which was scarce in the past, is the "money" fish. Along with flounder, perch, bluefish, and shad, they occupy fishermen who haul seines or drift or stake nylon gill nets. Making a net today involves "tying in" purchased "lease" (machine-made netting) to nylon top lines. First, the fisherman must choose lease with appropriate-size holes for the type of fish he wants to catch. Three-and-a-half-inch lease catches most desirable fish, and few undesirable ones. However, a fisherman who wants to have some "fun" catching the giant drum fish may choose a 10-inch lease. The fish swims part way through the hole and catches its gills in the net.

The fisherman next decides how much slack he wants in the net; generally, he wants more slack in cold weather. Then he will decide how much he wants the net to sink or float, and will add corks to the top and leads to the bottom accordingly.[156]

Knowledge of fish, tides, and weather will then determine when and where the fisherman uses the net. Many fishermen believe that different fish come on different winds. For commercial fishermen, Reeves recalls, a northwest wind generally meant a poor catch. A southerly or easterly wind, however, would bring, among other varieties, shad.

Fishermen still may "make a haul" with a hauling seine, but this method is less used than in the past, perhaps partly because, as Reeves recalls, it means "simply pulling your guts out!"

Either working alone or with one or two others, Reeves would put the seine out in a half circle from the shore and immediately pull it in. A strong ebb tide would make the haul more difficult by pulling the net away from him.

A good fisherman, Reeves claims, must stay ahead of the net. To minimize the tug of war with the tide, fishermen may haul seine "on top of the tide" at "high water slack," when the tide is not moving. Whenever they haul, however, if the fish are not moving they'll get only a "water haul."[157]

The final vagary with which the fisherman must deal is the market. "It's like I said, there's no happy medium for the buyers and the fishermen. He knows you got a product's gonna go bad. You can't eat it and you can't keep it, so you gotta take what you can get for it. I always said, they had a little shelf about six inches wide and they take their hand in their pocket, when you got a lot o' fish, and they throw the change up there and what hits there's what you get."[158]

Another creature that fishermen may pursue is the eel, and the pursuit is a full-time task from June through November. Eeler Lynwood Veach thinks nothing of following fish from 6 A.M. to 8 P.M. in the months when they are moving.

During that time, the eels feed and travel 24 hours a day, moving so quickly that an eeler needs a fast boat, a nimble body, and a good memory. Eels return annually to the same feeding spots, but the eeler will keep his eel pots well spread out and retrieve them regularly in his efforts to keep up with the eels.

Eels were caught more in the past, when spearing, dredging, and bobbing were legal. Searching the mud bottoms of clear streams for small entry holes, or probing in murkier waters with a rod, eelers could spear more than one eel at a time.

Handmade, split-oak fykes were also much used in the past. Today, most eels are caught in "pots" constructed on the same principle but of different materials, usually hardware cloth or wire mesh. Because the eel is "tem-

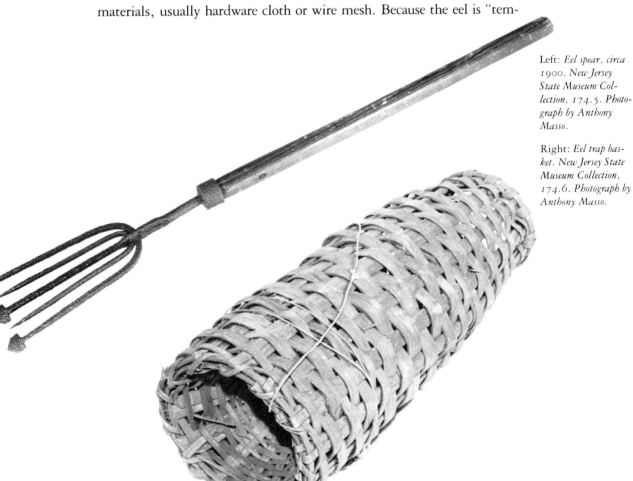

Left: *Eel spear, circa 1900. New Jersey State Museum Collection, 174.5. Photograph by Anthony Masso.*

Right: *Eel trap basket. New Jersey State Museum Collection, 174.6. Photograph by Anthony Masso.*

Opposite: *Making eel baskets, Greenwich. Photograph by William Augustine. Donald A. Sinclair New Jersey Collection. Special Collections and Archives, Rutgers University Libraries.*

peramental," according to Veach, he uses a wide range of variations in his pots: "Well, there's square ones; there's round ones. There's what I call the sea bass pot that are flat on one side, and there's quite a different variety. There's double funnel, with a long wire to go into where the net mesh is. Listen, if you could make a pot that would work everywhere and work all the time you could be a millionaire in a couple o' years." [159]

Like the lobster, the eel enters the pot tail first. To entice him to do so, eelers bait their traps with cut up horseshoe crabs containing eggs, or waste parts that local clam factories discard. Small eels, caught early in the season, are salted and sold as bait to crabbers. Larger ones are kept in a "live car," a small, boatlike box with an opening on top and screened ends to promote water circulation, until they are shipped by "live truck" to buyers in large cities. Locally, eels are usually smoked by individuals in makeshift smokehouses. Some oldtimers used to smoke fish in an old refrigerator mounted on cinder blocks, with a fire below, usually made of hickory, occasionally of sassafrass. [160]

Oystering and Clamming

Right by the Delaware Bay sits the small town of Bivalve, its name a reminder of the importance of shellfish to the area. As recently as the 1930s, residents claimed that "the whole world meets in Bivalve." Since the earliest days of settlement, coastal residents have built their lives around the harvest of oysters and clams. Oystering, particularly, has generated a distinct and elaborate folklife.

In Colonial days, oysters were gathered by hand with rakes or tongs. Some people continued tonging for oysters into the twentieth century, especially in the rivers. However, in the early nineteenth century the introduction of the oyster dredge launched the commercial oyster industry in Delaware Bay. The dredge originally consisted of a wooden crossbar with iron teeth to which was attached a rope mesh bag. After the Civil War, the dredge frame and mesh bag were made of iron. It was "drudged" along the bottom of the bay and then hauled in. The oysters were dumped on the deck and "culled," that is, separated into different grades by the crew. Crews were usually made up of men from the immediate region or immigrants who came from Philadelphia or who followed the dredging season up the coast.

The completion of the railroad to the Maurice River in 1876 made possible the shipping of oysters in refrigerated cars to markets in Philadelphia and New York. Prior to the 1920s, the oysters were shipped unshucked.

They were "floated" in wooden frames to keep them fresh and plump, and then moved with "oyster forks" by float crews into handmade wooden oyster baskets when they were sold. Carloads of the bivalves were shipped out daily by rail.

An oysterman's yearly cycle has always been built around the Delaware Bay practice of "planting" oysters. Small "seed" oysters that are raised on state-owned beds in less salty waters are dredged freely by licensed oyster boats for four weeks in May and transplanted to leased beds farther down the Bay. The seed oysters are left to grow until they reach a marketable size, which may take three months or a couple of years. Many of these leases have been held by one family for generations and may be named for an early owner. Fenton Anderson, for instance, who bought his leasing rights from Tulip Westcott, calls his lot the "Tulip Grounds." [161]

Dredging season traditionally began in September, quickened as the holiday season approached, and tapered off in January and February. In recent years, some oystermen dredge year round. Many oystermen, as befits the local title "oyster planter," farmed during the off season, while others worked in boatyards. Still others used their boats to fish, take out fishing parties, and haul freight, practices still followed today.

Under sail, boats would go out on Monday morning and return on Friday evening. Crew members, recalls John DuBois, would never bring a black suitcase aboard or use the word "pig," for fear of jeopardizing their journey. [162]

The crew was responsible not only for "culling" and shoveling discards over the side, but also for working the boat and dumping the dredges. The captain was a man well practiced in the art of tacking up and down as he dragged the heavy iron dredges over the oyster beds and raised them to the deck. His skill in maneuvering was a part of his reputation, as was his boat. Many oystermen reveled in the image of being tough, and this is reflected in their stories, such as the one about Elmer Tarburton.

Most of the towns along the Maurice River harbored oyster boats. A fleet of small sailing vessels called the "Mosquito Fleet" sailed out of Dividing Creek. These smaller boats could tong or dredge smaller beds and shallower waters.

In 1945, a prohibition against using power boats on oyster beds was lifted. Masts were removed, decks were rearranged, and a way of life was altered.

Today, though most of the oyster boats are survivors of the era of sail, they work in different ways. The crew usually numbers no more than four or five, for automatic dumpers and culling machines now separate most of the oysters and remove debris. The captain can run a power boat in slow circles to dredge the oysters. Boats go out early in the morning and return by

Tonging for oysters, Cedar Creek, circa 1910. Donald A. Sinclair New Jersey Collection. Special Collections and Archives, Rutgers University Libraries.

4 P.M. Because the oyster crop is smaller, dredging is done less often, and is more keyed to demand.

Since the 1920s, oysters have been "shucked" (opened) in shucking houses by oyster shuckers, who come mostly from Maryland and Virginia. After they are removed from their shells by hand, the oysters are "blown" to clean them in a vat, graded, and packed in metal containers that are then refrigerated.

Whereas oysters have been especially important to baymen on Delaware Bay, clams have been an important resource to their counterparts on Barnegat Bay.

Joe Reid of Waretown grew up on Barnegat Bay. He used to clam in the summer and build garveys in the winter, but for the past 10 years he has been building boats full time. In his day he clammed at numerous places in the bay. "I worked from Forked River to the Mullica River, which is at New Gretna, according to where the clams are and according to the weather. We don't stick to one spot." [163] Reid didn't use navigational charts; he knew the bay both from his own experience and from the traditional knowledge of other baymen, who have given places in the bay names such as Sammy's

Charles DeStefano of Pleasantville clamming on Barnegat Bay. Photograph by Joseph Czarnecki. PFP216651–11–14.

Slough (a place of deep mud), Buck's Channel, and Diamond Flat. "I don't know how they originally got their names. Since I was a kid, we just knew the names."[164]

Clamming is quite different from oystering. While oystermen transplant seed oysters onto their own leased beds, clammers go wherever they want to clam. Some clammers, however, lay their surplus in staked lots when the market for clams is poor. These lots are leased from the state and marked with corner stakes bearing the name of the clammer.

The Lenape Indians used to "tread" for clams and oysters; that is, they waded out into the shallow water to gather them. Today, clammers use two methods: raking and tonging. The most common rake is the Shinnecock, named after Shinnecock Bay on Long Island, New York. The rake is dragged along the bottom, often from the stern of the boat. Tongs, on the other hand, work like large scissors. They dig into the bottom to grab the clams, for clams burrow just below the surface, unlike oysters, which lie on the surface. The oldest tongs had wooden heads. Today the heads are made of iron and only the handles are wooden. Reid acknowledges that the iron heads are superior.

The garvey is essential for clamming with tongs, but not necessarily for raking. Reid explains why:

> The main object of a garvey for clamming is the fact that it lays still in the water. If you're tonging, for instance, you can't have a boat moving back and forth. You drop your tongs down and you feel clams, and the boat has to stay there so that you dig the clams out. If the boat moves, you can't get them out. Now with a rake—some of them use rakes off the stern—it doesn't matter. They drag these big rakes. Sort of a jerking motion. And then it doesn't matter what kind of boat you've got.[165]

Legendary tales are told about clammers, celebrating their skills, their knowledge of the bay, and their shrewdnness. Mr. Reid tells the following story about his brother.

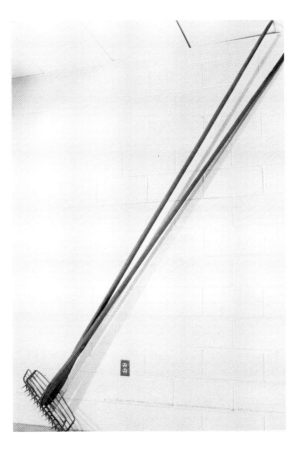

Clam tongs used by the Ridgway family in the early twentieth century. New Jersey State Museum, 81.99.4. Photograph by Anthony Masso.

Opposite: *Joe Reid of Waretown, garvey builder. Photograph by Joseph Czarnecki. PFP216395–1–22.*

My brother was always very particular about having his own spots, where he clammed. He didn't encroach on anybody. And he didn't like anybody to do it to him. Though this young fellow came out of the army and decided to go clamming. So they told him my brother was one of the best clammers. So naturally he followed him. And he followed him all day, and my brother would clam ten minutes here, ten minutes there, and he would move. So when they came in that night, he said to him: "How come they tell me you're the best clammer in the bay, and I followed you all day, and I didn't find anything." So my brother said to him, "Well, I know where they are, and I know where they ain't." And he said, "Today I've been clamming where they ain't." [166]

Fishermen, whether tonging shellfish or netting finfish, often cite their love of independence and the outdoors when they explain their attachment to their lifestyle. For some, it is an almost organic attachment, expressed in the desire to "die with salt in my ears."

Duck Hunting

The Barnegat Bay decoy and the duck hunting boat known as the "sneakbox" are both made of white cedar and are both adapted to the specific conditions of Barnegat Bay, a wide expanse of shallow water. "Many of the earliest late-nineteenth-century decoys from the Barnegat Bay area have long been admired for their similarity to small craft themselves," wrote folklorist Bernard Herman and archeologist David Orr.

The decoys of the Jersey shore, centering on Barnegat Bay, form a marvelous assemblage of artifacts. . . . They closely parallel the corresponding evolution in hunting boats developed in the same area. The premium was on weight and size since these commodities were in sparse supply on a twelve foot craft. . . . There was an additional desire for naturalistic realism for the hunting was on open expanses of water. . . . Outstanding examples of original design, the Jersey hollow duck or goose is not only formally symmetrical and cleanly carved and ornamented, but it is also an excellent solution to the combinative determinants of Bay ecology and small craft architecture. [167]

The sneakbox is a shallow-draft hunting boat, usually 12 feet long and 4 feet abeam, with a spoon-shaped bow and a melon-shaped hull. It is thought that the first sneakbox was made about 1836 by Hazelton Seaman

Barnegat Bay sneak-box, circa 1910. Made by J. Howard Perrine. New Jersey State Museum Collection, 70.156. Photograph by Joseph Crilley.

of West Creek. Originally they were either rowed or sailed with a sprit-rigged sail to the gunning grounds. Today they are powered by outboard motors or towed to the grounds by larger power boats. Some are still built as sailboats, used more for pleasure than for gunning. Those built for sailing have a centerboard trunk and centerboard. Those built for gunning have a rack on the stern to hold the rig of decoys.

Sam Hunt of Waretown makes his sneakboxes with white-oak timbers (frames), which he first softens by steaming them in a homemade steambox and then clamps into place on a model of the hull called a "jig." But, he explains, the original sneakboxes didn't have steamed timbers. Instead, they had frames which were sawed from large cedar logs. Hunt uses white cedar for the planks, because, he says, "I never seen a piece of it really rot in a boat. Never. It's light, and it will swell. You can put it together and leave the seams that far apart and it still comes tight. It won't leak." [168]

According to Hunt, the boat is called a sneakbox because it enables the gunner to "sneak up" on ducks. Actually, they were used quite differently, as decoy carver Ed Hazelton of Manahawkin told fieldworkers Tom Carroll and Nora Rubinstein. The hunter cut a V-notch in the meadow along the bay, and pulled his boat into it. The sneakbox was covered with brush, marsh elders, or hay, and the gunner sat facing the stern, waiting for the ducks to be lured down by the decoys. Today, Hazelton explained, it is more common for the gunners to use "gunning boxes" built with seats and shell shelves. They are more comfortable and can seat as many as six men.

Two different gunning traditions came out of the nineteenth century. One was that of the sportsmen gunners, usually wealthy individuals from outside the region, who hired local guides. The other was that of the market gunners, local people who made a living, at least in part, by supplying game for restaurants in nearby cities. The Federal Migratory Bird Act of 1918, which restricted wildfowl gunning to strictly regulated seasons, brought market gunning to an end.

In the nineteenth century, according to local historian Patricia H. Burke, the sportsmen traveled to Barnegat Bay by boat or stagecoach. After 1870, railroad connections to New York and Philadelphia made the trip much easier. The accommodations included boarding houses, hotels, and inns, such as the Chadwick House at Chadwick Beach, south of Mantoloking, and the Harvey Cedars on Long Beach Island. For the very wealthy, private gunning clubs were organized, including the Marsh Elder Gunning Club on Marsh Elder Island, the Manahawkin Gunning Club, and the Peahala Club.

Sometimes businesses maintained facilities for the use of their clients. George Heinrichs of New Gretna worked in a menhaden fish processing plant that maintained such a hunting lodge, and he sometimes would act as a guide. "We'd take them out for anywhere from a day to a week. They'd sleep at the lodge. We had a cook for the meals. . . . The lodge is torn down now. I went there in 1959 as a hunting guide, and I left in 1964–65. The lodge was torn down then."[169]

The local men who served as guides for visiting hunters would sometimes maintain small lodges for their own use. Milton R. Cranmer of Manahawkin, who was a guide from 1943 to 1957, leased the Flat Creek meadows near Marsh Elder Island for hunting. His father built a small clubhouse there and they nicknamed it "Cream Puff Castle."[170] Local hunters both built their own boats and carved their own decoys, because they couldn't afford the decoys made by the more prestigious carvers.

All Barnegat Bay decoys had certain characteristics in common. They all were made of white cedar, they all were hollow, and they all had painted, rather than carved, tail feathers. Within these parameters, four different styles developed along Barnegat Bay. The decoys from the "Head of the Bay" had a high tail with a small knob on it, a rounded bottom, a tight eye groove, and a rectangular lead pad on the bottom for ballast. The decoys from the town of Barnegat were similar, except that the tail was not as high, the bottom was not rounded, and the eye groove was less pronounced. The carvers from Parkertown made their decoys with a low tail and flat head. The ballast was made by pouring molten lead into a rectangular opening carved into the bottom, and an "ice-catcher" was carved behind the neck. The decoys from Tuckerton had a low tail, a round bottom, and ballast similar to that of the Parkertown decoys.[171]

Ed Hazelton said that the old carvers made all species of ducks, but mainly Canada geese, brant, black ducks, broadbills (scaups), canvasbacks, and redheads. The species depended on what the gunner wanted to gun for. The clubs gunned for broadbills, black ducks, and geese, because they were plentiful.

"The decoy as a historic artifact is basically a social tool," folklorist Bernard Herman has said. "It was used not [only] as an implement to lure birds, but as a status statement. One went into a resort hotel, got the finest guides, the finest sneakboxes, and obtained the best birds made by the best carvers in the area."[172]

Some of these prestigious carvers were Eugene Birdsall (c. 1857–1917) of Point Pleasant, Percy Grant (1864–c. 1960) of Brick Township, Jesse Birdsall (1843–1927) and Henry Grant (1860–1924) of Barnegat, Nathan Horner (1881–1942) of West Creek, Jay Cooke Parker (1882–1967) and Lloyd Parker (1858–1942) of Parkertown, and Harry V. Shourds (1861–1920) of Tuckerton.[173]

Harry Shourds's grandson, Harry V. Shourds, II, of Seaville, is carrying on the family tradition. He argues, however, that his decoys are different from his grandfather's and his father's decoys. He distinguishes between working decoys and decorative decoys, but he acknowledges that most of his decoys are made for collectors, rather than gunners. "Most people today buy them for decoration, but they're really a working decoy. They're what I think a duck looks like. I don't copy off a real duck, and none of the old-timers did. They hunted ducks and saw ducks in the wild, and took their memories with them. They worked from those memories."[174]

Harry Shourds judges a good decoy by how it behaves in the water:

For a decoy to be a working decoy, it has to look like a duck, float like a duck, and act like a duck in the water, the way it bounces and swims around. I think a decoy has to have enough roundness so that it will rock a little. It's got to swim back and forth. It has got to be weighted right so that it sits the right depth in the water, so when a duck comes over, he sees that more than he would see the shape of the duck. He sees it at a distance, say one hundred yards, and looks down and says, "That's a nice flock of ducks down there. Think I'll go down and see what they're doing." [175]

Carver Hurley Conklin was born in 1913 in Cedar Run, but for the past 40 years he has lived in Manahawkin. He made his first decoy in 1928, mainly for his own use. He reserves the term "decoys" only for those used by gunners. But, he says, "Today carvers, including myself, do not make decoys for gunners; they're too expensive."

For John A. Hillman, a gunner and decoy collector from Sea Girt, the traditions surrounding gunning are very much a part of place: "Each place, we gun different, just like neighborhoods. People are different in each neighborhood, and around Barnegat Bay this is what they've done over a hundred years." [176]

FARMLANDS

The following tall tale told by Tom Brown contradicts the image of the Pinelands as a "barrens" with poor soil for agriculture.

You know, that ground down there to Linwood is very rich. My friend Elwood Ford used to tell this story. "When we'd plant corn," he said, "Grandmother would make the hole for the hill of corn. Us children would drop it, then Dad would cover it up. Then he'd jump out of the way, the corn came up so quick. One day I was real brave. I grabbed ahold of it. I rode up in the air. I'd of starved to death, if Grandpa hadn't shot biscuits up there with a shotgun." [177]

Actually, there are a variety of Pinelands soil types, ranging from gravelly sand with almost no humus, too porous to retain water and fertilizers, and thus too poor for conventional agriculture, to fine sandy soil that holds fertilizers and is well suited for crops such as sweet potatoes, to sandy or gravelly loam with some heavy clay, that is good for fruit trees, but not wheat, rye, or other grain crops. Agriculturally, the region is divided into broad subregions: north of the Mullica River, where cranberries and blueberries have predominated; and south of the Mullica, where grapes, strawberries, sweet potatoes, and fruit trees have been grown.

In the eighteenth century, agriculture was a part-time activity in the Pinelands, second to lumbering, shipbuilding, and iron manufacturing. Farming was restricted primarily to the southern and coastal regions. The land was cleared by burning, a practice that was criticized by Count Julian Niemcewicz, who traveled through the region in 1799:

> Again sand and pine forests, the more sad because it was all burnt over. This tremendous damage is caused by indigent inhabitants who, having no meadows in which to feed their cattle, burn the woods. The fire running along the ground, turns the lower bushes to ashes; with this the earth is enriched and puts forth grass and other plants—in a word excellent pasturage for cattle. This advantage does not compensate for the harm done by the fires which rise from the lower growth to the tops and burn the taller and more useful trees.[178]

Cattle were allowed to graze on woodland pastures and on salt hay in meadows and on barrier islands. Early crops there included corn (maize) and rye, which were grown primarily for self-consumption.

Cranberry Farming

J. J. White saw the potential for agriculture in what had been previously thought of as "barrens." In 1916, he wrote:

> From the position it occupies, between the two great cities of the nation, it may be a marvel to some that this region should have remained so long uncultivated, but it is explained in few words. The soil is light and sandy, not suited to growing grass or the cereals, but yielding good crops when planted in small fruits. These, with the exception of cranberries, require easy and rapid facilities for marketing; such as are only obtained in the interior by the use of railroads, and those, until recently have been withheld. Hence, the swamps were left to make cedar, and the uplands to produce pine timber. But now, railroad facilities are being afforded, and large portions of "The Pines" are destined to become a fruitful garden under the skillful management of the fruit grower.[179]

The fruitful garden which White predicted, and which he himself helped to create, dazzles the eye with its color and the mind with its ingenuity. Out of acidic streams and sandy soils, cranberry farmers have built intricate waterways and fertile bogs. Cranberry agriculture is perhaps the best example of the resourcefulness and judicious adaptation that characterize Pinelands folklife.

The history of the development of the industry is a story of environmental recycling. The cranberry (*Oxycoccus macrocarpus*) is a vining evergreen that grows naturally in sandy swampy areas of eastern Massachusetts, the upper Midwest, and southern New Jersey. Its fruit ripens in the early fall and can be stored until spring. Natives gathered wild cranberries regularly before the 1800s, but the decline of other Pinelands industries—most notably the iron foundries—encouraged residents to adapt these natural resources to different uses in the cultivation of cranberries.

The first cultivated cranberry bog in the Pines was planted in the 1830s by Benjamin Thomas at Burrs Mill in Southampton Township.

In 1857, when James A. Fenwick purchased the 108 acres that would become the nucleus of the Whitesbog agricultural plantation, he was recycling the water supply and work force from nearby Hanover Furnace. As Mary Ann Thompson points out, the bogs themselves are "remodeled cedar swamps," the components of which—water, turf, and cedar—became reservoirs, roads, and flood gates.[180]

Eventually, Whitesbog would encompass 3,000 acres, most of them purchased between 1884 and 1909 by Joseph H. White, Fenwick's son-in-law. At the height of its development, Whitesbog consisted of cranberry bogs, blueberry fields, a water supply system, the village of Whitesbog that grew up around the sorting house, and the migrant workers' villages of Florence and Rome, named in honor of the Italian workers at the turn of the century.

Four parallel streams that flow from east to west into the Rancocas Creek, a tributary of the Delaware River, provided the water supply for Whitesbog. Gaunt's Brook and Antrim's Branch are located to the north and Cranberry Run and Pole Bridge are to the south. To the east and west are swamps. The main water supply came from the Upper Reservoir. The second water supply system was created by damming Pole Bridge Branch to form Canal Pond.

Between 1857 and 1912, 40 bogs covering 600 acres were designed and built at Whitesbog. Lower Meadow Bog, Old Bog, and Little Meadow Bog were the original bogs built by Fenwick. White built five other groupings of bogs, named the Cranberry Run Bogs, the Ditch Meadow Bogs, the

Pole Bridge Bogs, the Upper Reservoir Bogs, Antrim's Branch Bogs, and a grouping consisting of Big Swamp Bog, Billy Bog, and John Bog. Today it is more common for the bogs simply to be numbered.[181]

At Whitesbog, in the early twentieth century, J. J. White helped develop the process of adaptation to an art. In his manual on cranberry culture, he sketched out the recycling of "muck" into bogs.[182] And over the years, even the wild vines have been given second life, as growers continue to hybridize them, often sowing their own identity into the fruit with names such as Howard Bell, Richard, Garwood, Bozarthtown Pointer, Braddock Bell, Applegate, and Buchalow. The "bell" in some of the names refers to the bell-like shape of the cranberry; the names refer to the growers.

The engineering of land and water that are basic to cranberry farming begin with the location of the bogs on a good water supply. Most planters seek a ten-to-one ratio of headlands, or upland water supply areas, to bogs. Each of the cranberry plantations in the Pines today is located on a branch of a major waterway. A system of reservoirs, dams, canals, and dikes connects the bogs with the main water supply and acts as a system of valves and pipes which can be regulated as necessary with the gates that farmers build. [183]

The bog itself is a structure of symmetry and precision, and the present bog landscapes of the Pines represent many lifetimes of work. Today, cranberry farmers assess the fine points of various bogs and bog-building techniques, and even refer to some bogs, such as Buffin Meadows at the Darlington plantation, as "state of the art." [184]

As described by cranberry farmers Stephen Lee and Henry Mick, the building of a bog begins with planning for efficient water management. At a spot near a stream, the topography of the land is first surveyed, and the reservoir placed at the highest point. [185] The area in which the bog was to be built was formerly either scalped of its vegetation or flooded to kill the vegetation. Today the trees are usually removed with heavy machinery, and useless vegetation is burned off. Cedar and pine are kept for gates and equipment, cedar for things to be partly submerged and pine for things fully submerged. Irrigation channels, consisting of a main center ditch with perpendicular side ditches, were used in older bogs; today, underground pipes are used for irrigation. A dike surrounds the bog. It is made of a core of sand from the ditches that are dug around the bog, and it is covered with turf cut from the bottom of the bog to prevent erosion. These dikes also serve as narrow roads between the bogs. Wooden gates at key places in the dike walls control the flow of water.

The bottoms of older bogs may be uneven and rough compared with those of recently built bogs. Today, bogs are graded so that they are within a half inch of level for conservation of water and ease of harvest.

It may take three years to build a bog, and several more to develop the plants. Even then, a bog, like a house, may "settle" in places within the first year or two and require regrading.

Most new bogs are planted with cuttings from other bogs. A cover of sand is spread over the muck at the bottom of the bog. The vines are inserted in small holes in a grid pattern made with a long-handled tool sometimes called a "dibble."

Water is essential to the cranberry, not only as sustenance but also as protection. Thus, water levels in the bogs follow a pattern of response geared to both regular growth cycles and irregular temperature fluctuations. The "winter flood" protects vines from the cold of winter months, and the "spring draw" uncovers them for the growing season. At full fruition, the "fall flood" buoys the fruit for easy harvest. In between, water may play havoc if it turns to heavy ice and chokes off oxygen or if it appears as a spring rainstorm that inhibits pollination. Moreover, unseasonable drops in temperature can

Cranberries being picked by hand, Ocean County, 1877. Lithograph by Granville Perkins. From Harper's Weekly, *1877.*

damage uncovered vines. During frost season, according to Stephen Lee, Jr., "you don't plan to do anything in the evening. You have to watch the thermometer." [186]

The management of these floods and the surveillance of the dikes is entrusted to a "water foreman" whose credentials usually include mental maps of complex water systems compiled through a lifetime of living in the Pines.

Cranberry farmers have a history of independently crafting technology for their small, rather esoteric branch of agriculture. A. S. Doughty's description of hand picking in 1878 picturesquely illustrates the circumstances that would encourage the development of technology in the twentieth century.

A few days since it was the privilege of the writer to visit the cranberry bog of D. R. Gowdy, Esq., at Stafford Forge, distant one and one-half miles from West Creek, in Ocean County. . . . They were in the midst of gathering the crop, and the scene presented some novel features. Six or seven hundred pickers, comprising both sexes, were gathered from the surrounding neighborhood, some coming a long distance, and with their wagons scattered around suggested the idea of a gipsy encampment. The pickers formed a line, and each provided with handled basket of half bushel capacity, would gather the berries with remarkable dexterity, and average, for five or six hours, from two to four bushels in as many hours, and on a wager could pick twelve bushels in ten hours. The price paid per bushel for picking is forty cents.[187]

In the early twentieth century, the cranberry scoop was introduced in the Pinelands. The Makepeace scoop, which came from Cape Cod, and the Applegate scoop, which was designed by David Applegate of Chatsworth, provided the types on which other local scoop makers worked many variations. Basically, the scoop is a wooden box with one open side. Using the scoop requires bending low to the ground and "combing" the vines with light short strokes that do not tear the vines as the berries are pulled off. The operation was carried out as Doughty described, with scoopers strung across the bog, each worker having a one-peck box. When the box was filled, he would dump it into a one-bushel packing box and receive a chit from a field supervisor.

Cranberries being scooped, Hog Wallow, circa 1940. Photograph by William Augustine. Courtesy of the Donald A. Sinclair New Jersey Collection. Special Collections and Archives, Rutgers University Libraries.

Cranberry scoops were used until the 1960s, and they have now joined the ranks of other utilitarian objects, such as the decoy and the sneakbox, which have become aesthetic symbols of place. Joe Reid, whose wife, Gladys, is the grand-niece of David Applegate, makes replicas of the scoop to be used as flower holders and magazine racks.

Mark Darlington, great-grandson of J. J. White, says his father, Tom, can remember "back in the very old days" when everyone was on hands and knees raking with their fingers. Cranberry scoops represent a variation on that theme, as do many of the automated dry-pickers that have been used in this century, including one his father designed: "The way we picked these, now, before the wet-harvester became available, he had a small machine about the size of a desk that you walked behind that had rows of cones that would work in a dry bog, and it would sort of rake through the vines and flop up in a rotating bucket arrangement and then dump 'em in a bag in the back." [188]

Today only a few growers dry-harvest because it is less efficient, more time consuming, and more destructive to the vines than the wet-harvest. However, dry-harvested berries are preferable for fresh sales, so there is still a market for them.

In the early 1960s the "wet method" of harvesting cranberries was developed. The fields are flooded to a depth of at least two inches above the top of the vines, and special machines—either "walk-behinds" or "ride-ons"—agitate the vines, knocking the berries off. The berries float to the surface and are "hogged," or gathered, toward a conveyor belt that moves them onto a truck.

The wet-harvester is the subject of endless improvisation and adaptation which Darlington describes as "sort of a communal project." Because there are simply not enough farms to make the development of special cranberry machinery worthwhile to companies such as John Deere, the cranberry farmers pool their resources. Darlington describes how it may unfold:

> It's a very tight knit industry for the most part in terms of all the other locals. We can borrow equipment back and forth. . . . Dave Thompson, machining and fabricating, is fantastic at coming up with stuff that my dad can conceive of. . . . My dad will work out something and Dave will make it, and what'll happen is, somebody'll come up and look at it or will hear about it and we'll loan it to 'em and they'll try it out for awhile and they'll come back and say, "Well, we need this change or that change on it." And some grower can go to Thompson and . . . he can just make it up for them. [189]

Other exercises of ingenuity may involve the adaptation of commercial machines. Abbott Lee developed a cranberry pruner by adapting a John Deere Model 640 rake.

The packing house is the focal point of a cranberry plantation and the final point for technological innovation, set within a traditional frame. In the nineteenth century, harvested cranberries were transported from the bogs to the packing houses in covered wagons. The packing house was often located in a town, such as Medford or Vincentown, that was a good distance from the bogs. Later, as the workforce grew, so did villages, such as Whitesbog and Double Trouble, near the bogs and around the packing house.[190]

At the packing house, the berries were separated from the chaff. Then they were sorted by machines which operated on a "bounce" principle: good berries bounce; bad ones don't. Sorting machines bounce the berries as many as seven times. Legend has it that the bounce principle was discovered by Peg Leg John Webb when he dropped a box of berries at the top of a staircase.[191]

Cranberry sorting machine in operation. Courtesy of Everett Mickle and the Medford Historical Society.

Cranberry pickers. Courtesy of Mary Ann Thompson, Virginia Durell Way, and Cranberry History Collection.

A final sorting under sunlight was done before the berries were packed for shipping in barrels emblazoned with the special label of the grower. Often the label carried family nicknames. The American Cranberry Exchange classified berries and often assigned names of indigenous plants and places. These would appear on the label, also.

The traditional structure of packing houses evolved to accommodate these tasks. Their high-peaked, multiwindowed buildings allowed maximum light and ventilation.

Today, the berries arrive in trucks and depart in large, square boxes. In between, they must still be cleaned and sorted. Local ingenuity continues to rework machines to bounce the berries.

The development of cranberry agriculture dramatically affected the Pinelands population. In the nineteenth century, cranberries were harvested by local families. By the turn of the century, however, growing manpower needs brought about the recruitment of Italian workers from Philadelphia. Entire families were hired in September by a "padrone," or boss, who orga-

Abbott Lee, cranberry and blueberry grower of Speedwell, 1985. Photograph by David S. Cohen.

nized, transported, and oversaw the workers. Some Jews from the nearby Jewish agricultural colonies were also hired.

With the influx, villages grew up near the bogs. In recent times, however, the practice of housing migrant workers has given way to the hiring of day labor. Migrant blacks, Puerto Ricans, Haitians, and Cambodians have all worked the bogs, along with Anglo natives of the region. Many of the Puerto Ricans who used to migrate to the bogs have now settled into permanent communities at Woodbine, Hammonton, and Vineland. With the natives, they form the core of experienced bog workers.

George Marquez and Orlando Torres represent two different patterns in the lives of Puerto Rican agricultural workers. Mr. Marquez has worked for the past 20 years or more at the Birches Road Cranberry Farm in Tabernacle Township. He found the job through a friend who worked at the agricultural employment office. When he started, he told folklorist Bonnie Blair, he drove about 30 workers each day in a bus from Philadelphia. They hand-harvested cranberries using scoops. Only four or five of them were Puerto Rican. Today Marquez lives in Philadelphia. He works in the cranberry packing house only during September and October, using vacation time from his regular job in Philadelphia to work in New Jersey. [192]

Orlando Torres was born and raised in Chatsworth and now lives with his wife Hazel in Vincentown. His father was a crew foreman at the Haines's cranberry bogs, and he began working in his father's crew. Eventually, he himself became a crew foreman because he could speak both Spanish and English.

Most of Torres's crew are seasonal workers. They work for six months in New Jersey, picking blueberries in the summer and cranberries in the fall, and then they return to Puerto Rico. In Chatsworth, however, there is a permanent Hispanic population, which includes Torres's parents. Though his parents think of themselves as "Puerto Rican," Torres thinks of himself as a "Piney," a sentiment he proclaims on his "Piney Power" cap. He explained his feelings about the Pines to folklorist Bonnie Blair by comparing himself to the bird that leaves its nest before its time and will always come back, for, he says, quoting his father-in-law, "You can take the Piney out of the Pines, but you can't take the Pines out of the Piney." [193]

The cranberry families have created communities. At the center of the community of the growers are the families, many of which involve several generations working together. Often different aspects of the business are divided among members. His father, according to Mark Darlington, is the creative mastermind of machinery at Whitesbog. His brother, Joe, is the

Rev. E. H. Durell with a cranberry bouquet. Courtesy of Mary Ann Thompson, Virginia Way Durell and Cranberry History Collection.

manager, and Mark is the mechanic.[194] In the Lee family, Abbott oversees tasks such as development of techniques and machinery, and Stephen III handles marketing and management.[195] Wives and children are also integral to the farm. In smaller operations, they help with many of the chores of cranberrying.

The community of growers emerges from this nucleus of local families. The methods and machines that they trade are symbolic of the larger concerns that they share as growers. While each is guardian of the specific waterways that feed his bogs, all watch over the Pinelands water system at large. Their common problem of handling processed berries led many of them to form the Ocean Spray co-op 50 years ago. The practices of planting new bogs with shared cuttings and of burying a plantation owner with a bouquet of cranberries speak metaphorically of their shared identity.

Blueberry Farming

Many of the cranberry growers also raise blueberries. "Blueberries was a way of supplementing your income as it first came on," grower Brad Thompson of Vincentown told ethnobotanist Eugene Hunn, "so people would get enough money together to put in three rows of blueberries, and then they would get three more, and then they would get an old cranberry bog annd plant all that. And my grandmother's generation started that way."[196] Stephen Lee and his two sons Abbott and Stephen grow both cranberries and blueberries at Speedwell. "Our blueberry fields and cranberry bogs here are practically the same type of ground," says Mr. Lee. "In fact, we can turn any of the blueberry fields into cranberry bogs the way we're located. It's the same ground. If you've got good blueberry ground, you've also got good cranberry ground."[197]

Two varieties of blueberries grow naturally in the Pinelands: the highbush (*Vaccinium corymbosum*) and the lowbush (*Vaccinium pennsylvanicum*). Local residents refer to them as "huckleberries." In 1916, Dr. Frederick V. Coville of the United States Department of Agriculture, and Elizabeth White, the daughter of J. J. White, the founder of Whitesbog, attempted to cultivate blueberries in New Jersey. They enlisted the help of local gatherers to locate the best wild blueberry shrubs, and named many of the cultivated blueberries after the woodsmen who found them. The "keystone" of the cultivated blueberry, Miss White said in a 1953 interview, was the Rubel, named for Rube Leek of Chatsworth.[198]

Since that time many more varieties of blueberries have been developed through crossbreeding the original varieties. Some of the newer varieties are the June, introduced in 1930; the Weymouth, introduced in 1936; the Berkeley and the Coville, both introduced in 1949; and the Bluecrop, introduced in 1952.[199] Brad Thompson has grown all of these, but he took out the Covilles, because they weren't producing much, and he put in Weymouths, because, he says, they're sweeter than Bluecrop and Berkeley, they're a "good cropper," they get "good money," and you can get a tractor between the bushes.[200]

The propagation of blueberries is usually done from cuttings. The 12- to 30-inch-long shoots from which the cuttings are made are called "whips." The cuttings are collected in the spring, before the beginning of bud growth (usually between March 15 and April 10), and are planted in sphagnum-lined boxes containing peat and sand. In the early fall, the rooted cuttings are planted in the fields.

When the plant is one year old, it will flower and produce fruit. The flower buds are initiated in the summer and develop through the fall and winter. Coville advocated planting different varieties of blueberry bushes in alternating rows, because when the flowers are pollinated with pollen from the same variety, the berries are smaller and mature later.[201]

Blueberry scoop and picker's box. Lent by Mary Ann Thompson and Cranberry History Collection. Photograph by Anthony Masso.

The pollination is done by honeybees hired from beekeepers. Bob Reeves, a blueberry grower from New Lisbon, figures that it takes one hive per acre.

The beekeeper who supplies him takes his bees to Florida in the winter to pollinate orange and grapefruit trees, follows the blueberry blossoms from Carolina into New Jersey, and then the cranberry blossoms to Cape Cod. "You don't try to bring [the bees] in until there is bloom showing," says Reeves, "because if you bring them in too quick, they'll go out on to wild flowers." [202] The bees are left in the fields for three to four weeks. Stephen Lee notes that he hires bees first to pollinate his blueberrry bushes and a second time to pollinate his cranberry vines. "In other words," he says, "the same colony of bees is hired twice." [203]

The blueberries are usually harvested between June 20 and August 15. In the past, lowbush blueberries were harvested using a hand rake, sometimes called a "huckleberry knocker," similar to a small cranberry scoop. The highbush variety has usually been harvested by hand picking. Since the 1960s, growers have also used a mechanical harvester that straddles the row of blueberry bushes while hydraulically operated rods vibrate the bush to detach the fruit. Today, the hand pickers are either contract migrant workers or local high-school students.

There are two methods of hand picking. In the first, the berries are put into a small pail fastened to the picker's waist. The pail is then dumped into larger trays. In the second method the berries are picked directly into market boxes, which are transported on pallets to the packing shed to be processed for the fresh market. In the shed, the green berries, dirt, leaves, and sticks are sorted from the marketable berries by rolling them down a screen. Electric fans are now used to blow the leaves off the screens.

Impressions of the blueberry fields gathered while picking are captured in Margaret Bakely's painting of a blueberry packing house and field. Bakely and her husband Vernon live on the Thompson cranberry plantation in Vincentown. Years ago, Margaret tried to pick blueberries, but found that there is a knack to it that she didn't have:

> You've got to have big hands, or the berries will fall right through your hands. That's what happened to me. Some people could pick twenty trays a day, but I could only do a couple. You pick not with your fingers, but with your thumbs. You hold your hands like a cup, and go up to the bush and work your thumbs on them, and they drop into the cup. So the bigger hands you've got, the bigger the cup! [204]

Even more taxing than the task is the heat in a blueberry field, Bakely says: "You have to be able to stand the heat, and I couldn't."

Such strong impressions seem to have motivated by contrast the sense of

Blueberries being picked by hand. Photograph by Dennis McDonald. PFP235203–1–35.

Opposite: *Blueberries being unloaded at packing house. Photograph by Dennis McDonald. PFP235203-2-33.*

relief that Bakely reads in her painting. "I think of a warm autumn day—Indian summer—with the yellow sky reflecting the colors. And the crows. There are always lots of crows around. It's a feeling of rest after a busy summer."[205]

"When we're finished picking blueberries," said Stephen Lee, "we take about a week or ten days as a break, and then we bring in a crew of people that will prune blueberries for us."[206] The purpose of pruning is to balance the size of the fruit with the production of new fruit the following year. Too much pruning increases the size of the blueberries, but decreases total production; light pruning will result in more, but smaller, berries. Those who wield the shears have to know how to strike a balance. Vernon Bakely "used to be a great pruner," his wife recalls. "He picked it up from his mother. They'd go around and prune off patches together."[207] The pruning is done while the bush is dormant, and it is interrupted by the cranberry harvest in October. In November, pruning resumes and continues through the first week of April.

Many of the New Jersey blueberry growers are associated with the TRU BLU Cooperative, which was established in 1927. It accounts for about 20 percent of the total blueberry crop in the state. It represents both the large growers, such as the Haines, White, Reeves, Lee, and DeMarco families, and the small growers. Because blueberry growing is labor intensive, the small growers can continue to compete with the large growers. Brad Thompson feels that he has made a good living growing blueberries. "Of the natives," he told Eugene Hunn, "I know very few instances of abject poverty. There are still enough resources to keep a fairly good level of living, from what I've seen."[208]

Vegetable and Fruit Farming

In the last half of the nineteenth century, improved transportation led to the growth of agricultural towns at Egg Harbor City, Woodbine, Hammonton, Vineland, and Bridgeton, where crops were loaded on railroad cars or boats for shipment to markets and food processing facilities in Camden, Philadelphia, and New York. New crops were grown, including strawberries, blackberries, raspberries, grapes, sweet potatoes, apples, and peaches.

Strawberries were the first money crop in the region south of the Mullica River, where berry growing began on a commercial scale in 1861. By the turn of the century, blackberries, or dewberries, became more important than strawberries. Raspberries were a third important crop. The three were compatible, because they were grown in the same kind of soil, and because blackberries mature earlier than raspberries but later than strawberries.

Sweet potato harvest. Photograph by Joseph Czarnecki. PFP216422–1–6.

Hammonton became the strawberry center of New Jersey. Out-of-town buyers and commission agents went there to buy the berries directly from the farm wagons. In 1909 a farmers' canning company was organized in Vineland for canning strawberries, blackberries, tomatoes, and sweet potatoes.[209]

Grapes were another nineteenth-century crop. They were introduced by German farmers near Egg Harbor City and by Italians near Hammonton. The Italians grew them mainly for home consumption in a sour wine made by drawing off the liquor from pressed grapes. A grape juice factory was established in Vineland, but in 1911 only about 25 percent of its grapes were supplied by local farmers.[210] The Germans also initially raised grapes for home consumption, but by the 1870s wine production became the most important industry in Egg Harbor City. At that time there were more than 700 acres of vineyards in the Egg Harbor vicinity. Large stone vaults were built to store the wine.[211]

Unlike white potatoes, sweet potatoes (sometimes called "Vineland Sweets") were well suited to the sandy Pinelands soil. In the nineteenth century, potato fields were plowed with a one-horse plow and planted by hand, using a trowel or dibble. Harvesting, using potato forks, began about September first. The potatoes were gathered by hand and stored either in barns or cellars. There they were sweated by wood fires to raise the temperature to about 80° F. After several days the temperature was lowered, and the seed potatoes could be stored all winter in a dry place.

In the first decades of the twentieth century, new methods replaced old. The new farm machinery was at first horsepowered, and included two-horse plows, disc and acme harrows, and sulky cultivators. Today, tractors have replaced horses, but the equipment is similar.[212]

Today, Leonard Maglioccio of Middletown in Upper Township, Cape May County, explained to folklorist Jens Lund, a tractor pulls a harvesting machine called a "potato digger"; it digs into the ground and forces the yams to the surface. A farm worker sits on the potato digger and clears the vines away from the harvesting machines, while two other laborers on foot pick up the yams. Most of the yams are sold to a packing plant in East Vineland.[213]

In the 1930s and 1940s the peach crop was so important that Hammonton called itself "Peach City." Fruit farmers in South Jersey usually grew both peaches and apples, which are compatible crops. Peaches are harvested in the summer; apples in the fall. Compatibility is important, for it enables

the farmer to use the same machinery, keep the labor supply constantly active, increase his income, utilize land not good for peaches, and reduce the risk of relying on a single crop.

The peach harvest begins July 1 and lasts until September 10. Most peach farmers harvest their crop two or three times during the season. The picking is done by hand, using ladders and bags, and the peaches are put either in baskets or bins. Forklifts move the bins to the packing house.[214]

Peach farmer Ed Lamonaca's orchards are located in Hammonton near the farmlands his grandfather purchased after he immigrated from Italy. Lamonaca grew up there in a 15-room farmhouse shared with a large extended family. The families also shared the work of the farm.

They first raised peaches, then changed to apples, and then switched back to peaches. Lamonaca explained their reasons. A peach tree will survive 15 years, while an apple tree can survive 30 years or longer. However, apples are grown all over the country, whereas peaches require particular conditions that are not found everywhere. Furthermore, it is hard for South Jersey apple growers to compete with those of New York and Pennsylvania, and apples are picked through Christmas, while peaches bring in more money and sooner.

"The best thing for peaches," according to Lamonaca, "is a lot of fertilizer, high ground with a lot of good drainage, and constant water," the opposite conditions needed for blueberries and cranberries. Pruning is also good for peaches. "You don't want to put the energy back into making leaves. . . . You want your peaches on the outside of the tree, where the sun is." What's more, "you want to open the inside of the tree . . . and let the sun in." Both the peach and the tree are very delicate. The sun in the crotch of the tree and on the leaves makes the tree grow, he explained. "The tree likes hot weather. It likes Miami."[215]

Lamonaca thinks of the seasonal variations in the business as Mother Nature's way "of weeding out the amount of boxes as opposed to the amount of people." To avoid relying too heavily on a single crop, he plants cucumbers between his peach trees.[216]

Lamonaca believes that it would be impossible for someone to start an orchard from scratch today because peach orchards involve a great initial investment and it takes at least three years for the trees to produce. It's a long term investment: "The only reason I'm farming is because my family had it," he says. "What you're doing is you're trying to create something for your children, so that you can pass it down to them . . . even though they might not be interested in farming."[217]

Ed Lamonaca sorting peaches in packing house, Hammonton. Photograph by Dennis McDonald. PFP233374-4-10.

The South Jersey Wagon

Crops were brought to regional markets in South Jersey wagons, a wagon type similar in appearance to the more famous Conestoga wagon of Pennsylvania, which became the covered wagon of the American West. Both can be traced back to the English farm wagon, which, according to folklorist J. Geraint Jenkins, is derived from the Dutch wagon.[218] Both have a two-part undercarriage, consisting of a forecarriage and rearcarriage connected by a shaft called the "coupling pole." In both, the rear wheels are larger than the front wheels.

South Jersey wagons were used in the Pinelands to haul iron products from the furnaces, salt hay to the glass and paper factories, and cranberries to the sorting houses. The body of the wagon could be changed to fit the job. Often they were covered with canopies, like the Conestoga wagons. In 1830 it was reported that Burlington County had 977 "covered wagons."[219] In 1857 Colonel James A. Fenwick, the original owner of the cranberry bogs that became Whitesbog, described how these wagons were lined up during the cranberry harvest. "There have been seen at one time as many as sixty covered wagons with horses hitched to trees around the edges of these meadows. These wagons brought farmers' families who were busily engaged in picking cranberries."[220]

Most South Jersey wagons were made by local wagonmakers, wheelwrights, and blacksmiths. Wagons were usually named after the person who made them or the town in which they were made. In 1845, local historian Isaac Mickle wrote about the famous Pine Robber William Giberson: "It was said that at a running jump he could clear the top of an ordinary Egg Harbor wagon."[221]

Wagons were still being made in the first decades of the twentieth century. One of the many South Jersey wagonmakers was H. B. Ivins of Medford. In 1913 he advertised in a Burlington County farm directory as follows:

H. B. IVINS

Practical Wagon Builder and Horse Shoer

JOBBING A SPECIALTY

Painting and Lettering by Experienced Hands,

Trimming and Wheelwright Work.

Agent for Handford's Balsam

of Myrrh and Snow Flake Axle Grease.

Bell Phone 64–2   Branch Street, Medford, N.J.[222]

The farm market wagon owned by Byron T. Roberts of Moorestown was similar to wagons made by C. T. Woolston of Riverton and William Frech of Maple Shade. Frech made all kinds of wagons, a potato sorter, and commercial car bodies. His farm market wagon was called a "Frech Underslung." He advertised that "the word 'Frech' on a wagon is like 'Sterling' on silver, it is a mark of quality, it stands for the best of everything."[223]

Ivins's wagonmaking shop, Medford, circa 1910. Courtesy of Everett Mickle and the Medford Historical Society.

Ethnic Agricultural Communities

A long succession of ethnic groups has been associated with farming south of the Mullica River, including Germans, Russian Jews, and Italians in the nineteenth century, and blacks and Puerto Ricans in the twentieth.

The Germans settled near Egg Harbor City. The city was planned by the Gloucester Farm and Town Association, a Philadelphia-based organization founded in 1854 to resettle German-Americans from the cities in rural areas. The association purchased 30,000 acres in the Gloucester Furnace Tract, 5,000 in the Batsto Tract, and 1,000 additional acres.

Located on the Camden and Atlantic Railroad line in Atlantic City, Egg Harbor City was laid out in 1854. Each share of stock entitled the holder to a 20-acre farm and a building lot in town. The town's German heritage was evident in street names such as Cologne and Heidelberg and calendrical festivals, including a Weinfest, a Winzerfest, a Weinlesefest, and an Oktoberfest. In 1856 a monthly newspaper, the *Independent Homestead,* began publication in both German and English.[224]

Between 1880 and 1890 a large number of Italians settled in the Hammonton area. Located on the Camden and Atlantic Railroad, Hammonton was developed by Charles K. Landis, a lawyer, and Richard J. Byrnes, a banker. Landis went on to found the city of Vineland, but Byrnes remained in Hammonton. Believing that Italians were the best farmers, they sought to interest Italian immigrants in settling in both Vineland and Hammonton by means of agents and advertisements. Some of the immigrants came from cities such as New York and Philadelphia; others came directly from Italy.

Sometimes a large number of immigrants would come from a single town. After the Campanello brothers from Gesso, Sicily, settled in Hammonton, for instance, they were followed by many other immigrants from the same town. Neapolitans and Calabrians also settled in Hammonton. The Tell family, for instance, came from Naples in about 1870 and became prosperous berry farmers. At first the Italians from these various regions of Italy remained apart from each other, but eventually they developed an Italian-American community that shared such traditions as the Festival of Our Lady of Mt. Carmel, which is still held on July 16th in Hammonton.

Many of the farm laborers around the turn of the century were Italians brought in from Philadelphia and New York by padrones, who were paid a certain amount per laborer. The farmers met them at the train station and took them to the farms in wagons. The padrone usually remained in the city and left the supervision of the work to a crew member called a "row boss."

Many other Italians bought farms. Most of them grew the same crops as those grown by other groups, except for Italian beans and peppers. The pepper industry began, in fact, when Italian farmers started shipping a few of the peppers they had raised in their gardens to friends in Philadelphia. By the 1890s it became an important crop, especially in the vicinity of Newfield in Gloucester County.

These farmers marked the landscape as Italian in various ways. To bake bread, Italians in the Hammonton vicinity built outdoor beehive bake ovens fired by brush, roots, and even raspberry canes cut from the berry patches.[225] Around Vineland, farmers sometimes marked the boundaries of their fields with grapevines.

In the late nineteenth century, several Jewish agricultural colonies were established in South Jersey. The experiment was motivated partly by the Russian Jewish tradition of agrarian idealism, out of which Zionism developed, and partly by the desire of Jewish philanthropists to resettle Jewish immigrants from the urban ghettos in rural areas.

The first colony was Alliance, founded in 1882 in Salem County, three miles west of Vineland. It was organized by the Jewish Emigrant Aid Society, based in New York. Its members established a cigar factory and a shirt factory as well as farms. Alliance was followed by Rosenhayn, Norma, Carmel, Mizpah, and Woodbine. Only Woodbine, in northern Cape May County, is located within the boundaries of the Pinelands National Reserve.

Established in 1891 by the Baron de Hirsch Foundation, the philanthropic organization that supplied the funds for the Jewish Emigrant Aid Society, Woodbine became the largest and most widely known of the colonies. Although it was intended to be an agricultural colony, it developed instead as an industrial center with factories making clothing, hats, hardware, and machinery. In 1894 an agricultural school was also established there.

By 1901 there were approximately 3,300 Jewish farmers in these agricultural colonies.[226] They raised the same kinds of crops as their German and Italian neighbors, including strawberries, blackberries, and, later, grapes, sweet potatoes, and fruit.

These new immigrants faced not only the difficult circumstances of agricultural life familiar to all farmers, but also some unique to the new colonies. Many of these settlers had never farmed before, and so were just learning agriculture at the same time that they were trying to support themselves with it. Moreover, the acreage on which they were settled was in many cases uncleared and uncultivated.

Enterprises such as the clothing factories and institutions such as the Woodbine Agricultural School were established to help the colonists sustain themselves. While developing their knowledge of farming, they worked for others to bolster their often meager farm income.

"I started to earn my bread and butter when I was two years old," claims Bluma Purmell, who is the daughter of Moses Bayuk, one of the original founders of Alliance. Life on the farm was very hard, and Bluma recalls that Jewish families would often do day labor on other farms. This work included scooping cranberries in nearby bogs, a scene she has depicted in one of her many paintings.

Bluma's paintings provide a picture of life in the Jewish agricultural colonies, filtered through memories in old age. Vivid details of both the daily life and its larger meanings are distilled in her pictures. The cranberry bog, she recalls, belonged to the Petersons. While helping pick cranberries there with her father and sister, Bluma received her first lesson from her father on how to properly take care of things: "I ran in front of my father. I had my little tin cup, and I started picking berries. Then my father said, 'You go follow behind me and get the ones I miss.' From that I learned to always finish things up carefully."[227]

This philosophy of her father motivated Bluma in the many activities of her full life. At the age of 83, after a long career as a nurse and a nursing home administrator, Bluma took up painting. Her subjects include the family farm and farm chores. In 1981, with the help of Felice Lewis Rovner, she published her memoirs under the title *A Farmer's Daughter: Bluma*.

Other forms of the visual arts also depict the circumstances of the early years in the Jewish colonies. The Crystal family, who farmed in Norma, named their homestead "Tall Weed Farm," good-naturedly recalling the poor condition it was in when they acquired it. Martha Crystal has commemorated that name and scenes of their daily life there in an embroidered picture that hangs in the kitchen of their farmhouse.

Like other immigrants, those of the Jewish agricultural colonies became

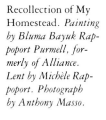

Recollection of My Homestead. *Painting by Bluma Bayuk Rappoport Purmell, formerly of Alliance. Lent by Michèle Rappoport. Photograph by Anthony Masso.*

experts at adapting. When they were joined after World War II by approximately 1,000 Jewish survivors of the Holocaust, many of them turned to the burgeoning field of poultry farming. The new immigrants settled in Farmingdale, Toms River, Lakewood, and Vineland. In 1951 the Jewish Poultry Farmers' Association was founded, and Vineland became known as the "Egg Basket of the East." [228]

By the 1970s, however, two major changes brought the era of the colonies to an end. First, the huge technological poultry operations of the South forced the smaller New Jersey operations out of business, and second, many of the younger generation had become well educated, as their parents had hoped, and entered professions. Another migration took place as they moved from the farms to the suburbs and cities.

Today, when reunions are held for those who lived in the Jewish agricultural colonies, they come from all over the country.

Beginning in the 1930s, blacks from Florida, South Carolina, and Georgia replaced Italians as seasonal agricultural workers. About half of them brought their families with them as they followed the harvest north-

Poultry farmers, Cumberland County. Photograph by Harvey W. Porch. Courtesy of the Donald A. Sinclair New Jersey Collection. Special Collections and Archives, Rutgers University Libraries.

ward through the South and into the Middle Atlantic States. They generally traveled with a crew leader in the crew leader's bus; however, some, known as "free-wheelers," came in their own cars. Their stay in New Jersey typically lasted four months. Accommodations were provided for them on the farms on which they worked. Most returned south for the winter.

By 1967, southern blacks were no longer the major component of the seasonal farm work force, having been replaced by Puerto Rican workers. In 1947 the Puerto Rican Department of Labor initiated a migration plan with the federal, state, and local authorities that established a uniform contract for agricultural workers from Puerto Rico. Most of these workers were men between the ages of 20 and 34. They were recruited by the Puerto Rican Department of Labor and flown on chartered planes to either New York City or Millville, from which they were transported to the Glassboro Service Association Camp, which had been established at an old WPA camp in 1947. Within 24 hours, they were usually assigned to a grower, generally the same grower each year.

Unlike the black migrant workers, who brought their families with them, the Puerto Rican workers usually left their families at home, returning to them after a stay of about five months in New Jersey.[229] Some of the Puerto Ricans have stayed in this country and established communities in Hammonton, Woodbine, and Vineland.

Domestic Life of the Farm

"Just because you plant it doesn't mean it's going to grow. . . . It means you're going to be out there working all the time!"[230] Hard work is a common theme of the oral histories of farming people such as Rae Gerber, whose family tree springs from far back in the history of Burlington County agriculture. Many of the traditional aspects of farm life derive from the demands and risks involved in farming. The structure of the yearly round, methods of thrifty resource use, and participation in communal work events are all ways of surmounting the difficulties of an agricultural lifestyle.

Just as a trapper organizes his year around the seasons of the animals he harvests, a vegetable farmer follows a calendar charted by the growing seasons of his crops. In South Jersey, preparation of fields for planting begins as soon as the soil thaws, usually in March. Planting follows, closely keyed to weather. Modern agricultural science records frost dates to guide planting schedules. Most farmers, however, also pay close attention to lunar cycles. Long experience shows that frost often occurs around a full moon, therefore they will avoid planting especially tender crops at that time. A farmer is guided in his planting routine by the accumulated wisdom of his own and his parents' experience in farming. Sometimes, other domains of life are incorporated into these practices; for instance, Italian farmers around Vineland used to say that peas planted on St. Guiseppe's Day (March 19) would flourish.

With the spring planting season, the busiest part of the year begins. During the summer and fall harvests, other activities are of secondary importance. Once winter cold sets in, the farmer's life slows down, but it is still busy with maintenance and repair of buildings and equipment.

Like Rae Gerber, who knows that "just because you plant it, doesn't mean you're going to get a crop," those who produce most of what they live on take care to see that resources are fully used.[231] This philosophy has traditionally been couched in the saying that is used to describe the preparation of meat from a butchered hog: "We use everything but the squeal." It is equally apparent in other foodways practices in the region.

Home canning and freezing have been important among many families, both those currently involved in farming and others, such as George and Helen Zimmer, who no longer farm but who have relatives and friends who still do. Folklorist Susan Samuelson observed that a cycle of reciprocity sees to it that nothing is wasted. Helen Zimmer receives fresh produce from members of her wide family network in the region. She spends a good deal of time processing the food in summer and fall, with the result being "well stocked freezers and cellar shelves lined with jellies, canned fruits and vegetables, stew mixes, purees, homemade wines, pickles, sauerkraut, and the like." These preparations are then shared with the original benefactors in an efficient meshing of natural and cultural resource management.[232]

Italian families often have "can houses," summer kitchens used especially for cooperative sessions of canning when all the women of the family work together to process large amounts of produce and to share it.

Communal work sessions provide two important resources: many hands to lighten the task and companionship to brighten it.

The hog killing was an annual late fall event in the past. At a hog killing, families would help each other butcher and prepare the meat from a hog. Each age and sex group had a job. The men did the work of butchering, with the younger men responsible for lifting and moving the heavy carcass. The women took care of the preparation of the meat and of a meal for the participants, with the oldest women doing the job of preparing the sausage casings since they could do it seated. The children ran errands.

The slaughtered hog was dipped into a tub of scalding water before the

Opposite: *Helen Zimmer of Egg Harbor City preparing chow-chow. Photograph by Elaine Thatcher. PFP215661-3-25.*

Following overleaf: *The Sew and Sews of the Tabernacle Methodist Church. Photograph by Dennis McDonald.*

hair and bristles were scraped off the skin. Then the various parts were prepared. The liver of the hog was often cooked that day to feed the group. Fatty scraps were rendered for lard, and hams were cut to be cured. Ground sausage mixture was prepared from scrap parts and stuffed into casings made from intestines that had been scraped, rinsed with running water several times, and turned inside out. Often, the sausage was divided among the participating families. Other parts were salted and stored on an upper floor of the house.[233]

Quilting has traditionally been another important activity whose rhythm is set by natural cycles. In South Jersey, where asparagus is a first crop for many farmers, the quilting season spans the winter and halts in April or May when it is time to pull asparagus. The Sew and Sews quilting group of Tabernacle Methodist Church has met weekly for 50 years in Rae Gerber's home in Tabernacle. They quilt the pieced tops that members make or others bring them, often completing as many as 25 quilts a season. The income from their work helps support the church.

However, such "bees" are a remnant of an era when all bedcovers were handmade and many hands were needed to get the task done. Other traditions surrounding quilting are recalled by Mrs. Gerber, who counts several seamstresses among her great-aunts.

To hone her sewing skills, a young girl made 12 quilts before her marriage. Upon her engagement she began the thirteenth, her bridal quilt. Mrs. Gerber still has the bridal quilt made in 1856 by her grandmother, Rachel Evans, for her marriage to Jesse S. Braddock. Like most of her other historic quilts, it is large—approximately three yards square—thin, and light. A thin, warm layer of wool forms the interfacing. Rachel Evans's wedding quilt is in a pattern similar to one called "Ocean Waves," yet is distinct in that the pieces are square rather than triangular. The quilting is in a feather and rose stitch.[234]

According to Mrs. Gerber, other patterns popular in the region in the past were the Oakleaf and Reel and the Album. Her collection includes one of each of these made by her forebears. The Album quilt is signed by many friends and relatives of Rachel Evans from the Medford area. In the 1970s, the Tabernacle group made a signature quilt from an historic Tumbling Block pattern. It bears the names of all the donors to the Tabernacle Historical Society fund drive, making it a colorful statement of people and place. Most of the names are of Tabernacle families.

Rachel Evans's quilts were probably stitched on the same frame that Rae Gerber and her friends have worked around for so long. It was made in the 1840s by one of the members of the Braddock family, with sturdy walnut posts and "Jersey iron rings that will never rust."[235]

In addition to making good use of womanpower, quilting makes economical use of materials. In the past, scraps from other sewing projects were stitched into quilt tops. Mrs. Gerber still has boxes of such materials, from which she would choose colors and patterns most pleasing to her taste. Other quilts made use of the colorful cloth used for feedbags before World War II. In more recent times, she has purchased fabric specifically for her quilts.

For Rae Gerber, the best patterns are the more difficult ones, such as the Rolling Star. These occupy the hands and entertain the eye. "My hands have to be busy," she says. But undirected or imprecise busy-ness is not sufficient. As if speaking for all women who have made beautiful and precise functional pieces, Rae Gerber says, "If you're going to put something together, why not make it beautiful while you're doing it, rather than slap it together haphazardly."[236]

Though a quilt warms, decorates, and occupies, its most eloquent function is expressiveness. The quilts Rae Gerber has made for each of her grandchildren on the occasion of his or her wedding, each of different design, speak not only about the individuality of the offspring and the creativity of the grandmother, but also about the continuity and importance of the family.

CONCLUSION

Environmentally, the New Jersey Pinelands is a special place. It is a wilderness in the midst of the megalopolis, and the repository of a large underground supply of fresh water. It marks the northernmost range limits for certain animal and plant species, and the southernmost limit for others, and is the habitat of some endangered species, such as the Pine Barrens tree frog. It is the first National Reserve in the United States. This specialness is recognized in the words of the Pinelands Commission Management Plan: "No other area has the same pattern of natural habitats, distribution of plant and animal populations, and unusual variety of plant and animal species."[237]

Yet in other ways it is similar to other places. Many of the products and industrial activities of the Pinelands can be found elsewhere. Lumber and shipbuilding supplies have been produced from the pine woods of North Carolina, and iron has been forged in the forests of Pennsylvania. Cranberries have been harvested from the bogs of Cape Cod, and clams have been gathered commercially from the bays of Long Island. Some of the methods used in those places have been adopted here, as well—the wet-harvesting of cranberries, for instance, which was developed in Massachusetts.

Even the stereotype of the "Piney" is not unlike that of isolated people elsewhere in the United States, such as the Southern Appalachian mountain people, and it has the same roots as that stereotype. Conversely, the reversal of that image, embodied in such slogans as "Piney power," is similar to the way that Americans of an earlier day took the comic image of the Yankee and turned it into a positive figure of national pride.

What makes the Pinelands distinct is the particular interaction of the people with their special environment. They have gained intimate knowledge of it over the years and have used their knowledge both to shape the landscape itself and to create their folklife.

The landscape has not always appeared as it is today. A rural industrial area became a wilderness, barrens became rich farmlands, and a hinterland became a popular recreational center. Each of these changes was wrought by residents using their knowledge of place to develop resources. While some of the uses have been destructive, such as the depletion of the woodlands to fuel nineteenth-century industries, others have been constructive. Sand has been processed into glass; cranberry bogs have been built from swamps. Folk technologies have made some of these transformations of the landscape possible.

In addition to creating such technologies, the people of the Pinelands have used their intimate knowledge of place to create many other folklife forms. They have shaped artifacts tailored to their environments: schooners designed for the special conditions of Delaware Bay and sneakboxes superbly suited to Barnegat Bay. Some artifacts are themselves bits of the environment reshaped, such as evergreen grave blankets and decoys. The people shape and transform the environment in other ways when they create art forms. Their special vision and deep attachment infuse their songs and stories, their paintings and carvings. These forms reveal the Pinelands that residents experience.

While there are many ways to understand the Pinelands, its folklife is one of the best.

NOTES

1. R. Alan Mounier, "A Study of Waterpowered Sawmills in the Pine Barrens of New Jersey," in *Historic Preservation Planning in New Jersey,* ed. Olga Chesler (Trenton: Office of New Jersey Heritage, 1984), 93.

2. Interview, Eugene Hunn with Jack Cervetto, June 22, 1984, PFP84–AEH014, Pinelands Folklife Project Archive, American Folklife Center, Library of Congress. Hereafter, references to archive materials will be listed with names, data retrieval number, and date only.

3. Interview, Jens Lund with George Brewer, October 15, 1983, PFP83–RJL008.

4. Interview, Eugene Hunn with Jack Cervetto, March 18, 1984, PFP84–AEH006.

5. Hunn with Cervetto, PFP84–AEH014.

6. Interview, Eugene Hunn with Jack Cervetto, March 18, 1984, PFP84–AEH002.

7. Hunn with Cervetto, PFP84–AEH006.

8. Hunn with Cervetto, PFP84–AEH002.

9. Herbert Halpert, "The Piney Folk Singers," *Direction* 2 (1939):15.

10. Henry Glassie, "William Houck: Maker of Pounded Ash Adirondack Pack-Baskets," *Keystone Folklore Quarterly* 12 (1967):40–42.

11. Agreement of Brotherton Indians to Sale of Land at the Brotherton Reservation, January 15, 1802, New Jersey Division of Archives and Records Management, Trenton, N.J.

12. U.S. Census, 1880, Burlington County, Shamong Township (manuscript).

13. Will of Ann Roberts, August 7, 1894, Will 21042C, N.J. Division of Archives and Records Management, Trenton, N.J.

14. *Mt. Holly Herald,* 15 April 1932, 3.

15. Harry B. Weiss and Robert J. Sim, *Charcoal Burning in New Jersey from Early Times to the Present* (Trenton: New Jersey Agricultural Society, 1955), 9–12.

16. Interview, Mary Hufford with Harry and Gladys Payne, November 14, 1983, PFP83–RMH032.

17. Weiss and Sim, *Charcoal Burning,* 20–33.

18. Ibid.

19. Henry H. Bisbee and Rebecca B. Colesar, eds., *Martha: 1801–1815: The Complete Furnace Diary and Journal* (Burlington, NJ: H. H. Bisbee, 1976), 63.

20. Mary Hufford, "Folk-Artists-in-the-Schools Final Report," (New Jersey State Council on the Arts, 1980).

21. John R. Stilgoe, *Common Landscape of America, 1580 to 1845* (New Haven and London: Yale University Press, 1982), 268–274.

22. Charles S. Boyer, *Early Forges and Furnaces in New Jersey* (Philadelphia: University of Pennsylvania Press, 1931), 2–9;

Arthur D. Pierce, *Iron in the Pines* (New Brunswick: Rutgers University Press, 1957), 10–19.

23. Bisbee and Colesar, *Martha,* 12–13, 17–18, 25, 62–63.

24. Boyer, *Early Forges and Furnaces,* 174–190; Pierce, *Iron in the Pines,* 117–155.

25. Quoted in Pierce, *Iron in the Pines,* 35–37.

26. Mary Hufford, "Navigators in a Sea of Sand" (Pinelands Folklife Project, 1985), 210.

27. Interview, Rita Moonsammy with Anne Salmons, March 15, 1985.

28. Ibid.

29. Hufford with Payne, PFP83–RMH032.

30. Herbert Halpert, "Folk Tales and Legends from the New Jersey Pines: A Collection and a Study" (Ph.D. dissertation, Indiana University, 1947), I:240–241.

31. Michael Fowler and William A. Herbert, *Papertown of the Pine Barrens: Harrisville, New Jersey* (Eatontown, NJ: Environmental Education Publishing Service, 1976).

32. Adeline Pepper, *The Glass Gaffers of New Jersey* (New York: Charles Scribner's Sons, 1971), 60–65, 313–315.

33. Interview, Rita Moonsammy with Dorothy Lilly, April 13, 1982.

34. Ibid.

35. Interview, Rita Moonsammy with Malcolm Jones, April 26, 1982.

36. Moonsammy with Lilly.

37. Interview, Rita Moonsammy with Theodore Ramp, March 18, 1985.

38. Roy C. Horner, *Tempo: The Glass Folks of South Jersey* (Woodbury, NJ: Gloucester County Historical Society, 1985), 5–6.

39. Moonsammy with Lilly.

40. Interview, Rita Moonsammy with Walter Earling, April 21, 1982.

41. Donald Pettifer, "Glass Folk Art in New Jersey" in *The Challenge of Folk Material for New Jersey Museums,* (forthcoming).

42. Moonsammy with Ramp.

43. Ibid.

44. Yi Fu Tuan, *Topophilia: A Study of Environmental Perception, Attitudes, and Values* (Englewood Cliffs, NJ: Prentice-Hall, 1974), 105.

45. Interview, Mary Hufford with members of Harmony Gun Club, December 10, 1983, PFP83–AMH024.

46. Interview, Rita Moonsammy with Jack Cervetto, May 29, 1985.

47. Interview, Mary Hufford with members of the Spartan Gun Club, November 17, 1983, PFP83–RMH044.

48. Hunn with Cervetto, PFP84–AEH006.

49. Interview, Eugene Hunn with Tom Brown, December 1983, PFP83–AEH008.

50. Interview, Rita Moonsammy with Tom Brown, February 17, 1982.

51. Interview, Eugene Hunn with Tom Brown, October 10, 1983, PFP83–AEH002.

52. Jonathan Berger and John W. Sinton, *Water, Earth, and Fire: Land Use and Environmental Planning in the New Jersey Pine Barrens* (Baltimore: Johns Hopkins University Press, 1985), 123.

53. John Harshberger, *The Vegetation of the New Jersey Pine-Barrens: An Ecologic Investigation* (New York: Dover Publishers, 1970), 30.

54. Fieldnotes, Eugene Hunn, PFP84–FEH0618.

55. Ibid.

56. Interview, Rita Moonsammy with Hazel Landy, December 19, 1985.

57. Hunn with Cervetto, PFP84–AEH014.

58. Fieldnotes, Eugene Hunn, PFP83–FEH1011.

59. Susan Samuelson, "Christmas in the Pines" (Unpublished ms.).

60. Moonsammy with Landy.

61. James Still, *Early Recollections and Life of Dr. James Still, 1812–1885,* facsimile edition (1877; reprint, Medford, NJ: Medford Historical Society, 1971), 119–120.

62. Alvin T. M. Lee, *Land Utilization in New Jersey: A Land Development Scheme in the New Jersey Pine Area,* New Jersey Agricultural Experiment Station Bulletin no. 665 (New Brunswick: New Jersey Agricultural Experiment Station, 1939).

63. Gustav Kobbé, *The New Jersey Coast and Pines* (Short Hills, NJ: Gustav Kobbé, 1889), 86–88.

64. Ibid., 88.

65. Pierce, *Iron in the Pines,* 156–173.

66. Berger and Sinton, *Water, Earth, and Fire,* 80–83.

67. Interview, Rita Moonsammy and Mary Hufford with Valia Petrenko, October 21, 1983, PFP83–RRM001.

68. Robert C. Alexander, "The Shingle Miners," *Cape May County Magazine of History and Genealogy* 4 (1957): 99–104.

69. Ibid.

70. Interview, Jens Lund with Charles Pomlear, November 10, 1983, PFP83–FJL028.

71. Tom Carroll, "Final Report, Phase I" (Pinelands Folklife Project, 1983).

72. [Peter Kalm,] *The American of 1750: Peter Kalm's Travels in North America . . . ,* ed. Adolph B. Benson (New York: Wilson-Erickson, 1937) I:298–299.

73. Interview, Tom Carroll with Joe Reid, October 8, 1983, PFP83–ATC002.

74. Mary Hufford, "Culture and the Cultivation of Nature in the Pinelands National Reserve," in *Folklife Annual* I (1985): 10–39.

75. Interview, Tom Carroll with Joe Reid, October 8, 1983, PFP83–RTC001.

76. Fieldnotes, Eugene Hunn, PFP84–FEH0318.

77. Kalm, *Travels,* 299.

78. Hufford, "Navigators," 145.

79. Interview, Rita Moonsammy with Helen Zimmer, March 18, 1985.

80. Interview, Rita Moonsammy with the Frazee family, March 21, 1985.

81. Ibid.

82. Fieldnotes, Mal O'Connor, PFP83–FM01014.

83. Ibid.

84. Kalm, *Travels,* 300.

85. Hunn, PFP84–FEH0318.

86. Ibid.

87. Rev. Allen H. Brown, "The Character & Employments of the Early Settlers of the Sea-Coast of New Jersey," 1879, reprinted in New Jersey Historical Society *Publications,* 2nd ser., 6 (1879–1881): 41.

88. Interview, Jens Lund with George Campbell, November 7, 1983, PFP83–FJL023.

89. Harold F. Wilson, *The Jersey Shore: A Social and Economic History of the Counties of Atlantic, Cape May, Monmouth, and Ocean* (New York: Lewis Historical Publishing Company, 1953) II: 747.

90. Ibid.

91. Ibid., 748–51.

92. Interview, Jens Lund with George Campbell, November 7, 1983, PFP83–FJL024.

93. Interview, Rita Moonsammy with Ed Gibson, May 10, 1982.

94. Wilson, *The Jersey Shore,* 751.

95. Ibid., 748.

96. Lund with Campbell, PFP83–FJL023.

97. Ibid.

98. Moonsammy with Gibson.

99. Lund with Campbell, PFP83–FJL023.

100. Lund with Campbell, PFP83–FJL024.

101. Ibid.

102. Wilson, *The Jersey Shore,* 889.

103. Kalm, *Travels,* 76–77.

104. *National Standard and Salem County Advertiser,* 14 September 1853, p. 2, as quoted in Wilson, *The Jersey Shore,* 889.

105. Interview, Rita Moonsammy with Leslie Christofferson, March 6, 1985.

106. Ibid.

107. Ibid.

108. Ibid.

109. Interview, Rita Monsammy with Albert Reeves, June 3, 1982.

110. Ibid.

111. Ibid.

112. Kalm, *Travels,* 239–240.

113. Moonsammy with Brown.

114. Ibid.

115. Interview, Rita Moonsammy with Tom Brown, December 17, 1985.

116. Interview, Eugene Hunn with Tom Brown, June 21, 1984, PFP84–AEH009.

117. Berger and Sinton, *Water, Earth, and Fire,* 47.

118. Interview, Gerald Parsons with Kenneth Camp, October 2, 1984.

119. Interview, David Cohen and Rita Moonsammy with Kenneth Camp, September 19, 1985.

120. Interview, Rita Moonsammy with Albert Reeves, February 12, 1982.

121. Parsons with Camp.

122. Interview, Rita Moonsammy with Kenneth Camp, September 23, 1982.

123. Cohen with Camp.

124. Interview, Gerald Parsons with Albert Reeves, September 24, 1984, PFP84–RGP006.

125. Ibid.

126. Cohen with Camp.

127. Alonzo T. Bacon, *Recollections Pertaining to the Seafaring Life* (Bridgeton, NJ: The Evening News, 1970).

128. Glenn S. Gordinier, "Maritime Enterprise in New Jersey: Great Egg Harbor During the Nineteenth Century," *New Jersey History* 97 (1979): 105–117.

129. Brown, "Character & Employments," 17.

130. Gordinier, "Maritime Enterprise," 105–117.

131. Alan Frazer and Wayne Yarnall, "New Jersey Under Sail," *New Jersey History* 99 (1981):196.

132. Donald H. Rolfs, *Under Sail: The Dredgeboats of Delaware Bay* (Millville: Wheaton Historical Associations, 1971), 11.

133. Interview, David Cohen and Rita Moonsammy with John DuBois, October 19, 1983.

134. Berger and Sinton, *Water, Earth, and Fire,* 63.

135. Carroll, "Final Report," 4.

136. Interview, Tom Carroll with Joe and James Reid, October 8, 1983, PFP83–RTC001.

137. Moonsammy with Reeves, June 3, 1982.

138. Interview, Rita Moonsammy with John DuBois, February 19, 1982.

139. Carroll with James Reid, PFP83–RTC001.

140. Moonsammy with Reeves, June 3, 1982.

141. Fieldnotes, Tom Carroll, PFP83–FTC1007.

142. Carroll with Reid, PFP83–RTC001.

143. Interview, Rita Moonsammy with Belford Blackman, September 17, 1984.

144. Interview, Rita Moonsammy with Fenton Anderson, September 17, 1984.

145. Interview, Jens Lund with Louis Peterson, October 22, 1983, PFP83–RJL017.

146. Moonsammy with Reeves, June 3, 1982.

147. Interview, David Cohen with Todd Reeves, December 15, 1983.

148. Interview, Rita Moonsammy with Norman Jeffries, September 17, 1984.

149. Interview, Rita Moonsammy with Joe Reid, March 13, 1985.

150. Ibid.

151. Berger and Sinton, *Water, Earth, and Fire,* 58.

152. Moonsammy with Reeves, February 12, 1982.

153. Mary Hufford, "Maritime Resources and the Face of South Jersey," in *Festival of American Folklife Program Book,* ed. Tom Vennum (Washington, D.C.: Smithsonian Institution, 1983), 12–15.

154. Interview, Rita Moonsammy with Nerallen Hoffman, February 11, 1983.

155. Interview, Jens Lund with Louis Peterson, October 22, 1983, PFP83–RJL016.

156. Ibid.

157. Interview, Rita Moonsammy with Albert Reeves, December 19, 1985.

158. Interview, Jens Lund with Veach family, November 11, 1983, PFP83–FJL032.

159. Interview, Jens Lund with Veach family, November 11, 1983, PFP83–RJL029.

160. Lund with Peterson, PFP83–RJL016.

161. Interview, Rita Moonsammy with Fenton Anderson, February 8, 1982.

162. Moonsammy with DuBois.

163. Interview, Mary Hufford and David Cohen with Joe Reid, November 4, 1985.

164. Ibid.

165. Ibid.

166. Ibid.

167. Bernard Herman and David Orr, "Decoys and Their Use: A Cultural Interpretation," Academy of Natural Sciences of Philadelphia *Frontiers* 1 (1979):6–7.

168. Interview, Christopher Hoare with Sam Hunt, April 28, 1978, quoted in David Steven Cohen, *The Folklore and Folklife of New Jersey* (New Brunswick: Rutgers University Press, 1983), 122.

169. Interview, Elaine Thatcher with George Heinrichs, October 1, 1983, PFP83–RET009.

170. Patricia H. Burke, *Barnegat Bay Decoys and Gunning Clubs* (Toms River, NJ: Ocean County Historical Society, 1985), 25–37.

171. Ibid., 11.

172. Quoted in the documentary film, *In the Barnegat Bay Tradition*, produced by the New Jersey Historical Commission and New Jersey Network (1982).

173. Burke, *Barnegat Bay Decoys and Gunning Clubs,* 12–23.

174. Quoted in *In the Barnegat Bay Tradition*.

175. Quoted in ibid.

176. Quoted in ibid.

177. Interview, Rita Moonsammy with Tom Brown, June 4, 1985.

178. Julian Ursyn Niemcewicz, *Under Their Vine and Fig Tree: Travels Through America in 1797–1799, 1805 . . .* New Jersey Historical Society Collections, vol. 14 (Elizabeth, NJ: Grassmann, 1965), 217–218.

179. J. J. White, *Cranberry Culture* (New York: Orange Judd, 1916), 24.

180. Mary Ann Thompson, "The Landscapes of Cranberry Culture," in *History, Culture, and Archeology of the Pine Barrens: Essays from the Third Pine Barrens Conference,* ed. John W. Sinton (Pomona, NJ: Stockton State College, 1982), 193–211, as cited in Hufford, "Navigators," 112.

181. William Bolger, Herbert J. Githens, and Edward S. Rutsch, "Historic Architectural Survey and Preservation Planning Project for the Village of Whitesbog, Burlington and Ocean Counties, New Jersey" (Morristown, NJ: New Jersey Conservation Foundation, 1982).

182. White, *Cranberry Culture,* 29–35.

183. Berger and Sinton, *Water, Earth, and Fire,* 76.

184. Interview, Mary Hufford with Mark Darlington, November 1983, PFP83–AMH015.

185. Interview, Christine Cartwright with Haines, Henry, and Francis Mick, September 29, 1983, PFP83–RCCo11; Interview, Mal O'Connor with Stephen, Jr., Stephen III, and Abbott Lee, November 12, 1983, PFP83–RMO015, as cited in Hufford, "Navigators," 114–115.

186. O'Connor with Lee, PFP83–RMO015.

187. A. S. Doughty, quoted in T. F. Rose and H. C. Woolman, *Historical and Biographical Atlas of the New Jersey Coast* (Philadelphia: Woolman and Rose, 1878), 308.

188. Hufford with Darlington, PFP83–AMH015.

189. Ibid.

190. Thompson, "The Landscapes of Cranberry Culture."

191. Hufford, "Navigators," 111–112.

192. Interview, Bonnie Blair with George Marquez, October 14, 1983, PFP83–RBBoo1.

193. Interview, Bonnie Blair with Orlando and Hazel Torres, October 20, 1983, PFP83–RBBoo3.

194. Hufford with Darlington, PFP83–AMH015.

195. Mal O'Connor, "Time, Work, and Technology: A Multi-Generational Approach to Family Business in the Pine-lands" (Paper presented at American Folklore Society 1984 Annual Meeting, San Diego, California, October 14, 1984).

196. Interview, Eugene Hunn with Brad Thompson and Bob Reeves, June 22, 1984, PFP84–AEHo11.

197. Interview, David Cohen with Stephen Lee, Jr., October 16, 1985.

198. Quoted in Bolger, Githens, and Rutsch, "Historic Architectural Survey," 47.

199. Paul Eck and Norman F. Childers, *Blueberry Culture* (New Brunswick, NJ: Rutgers University Press, 1966), 65.

200. Hunn with Thompson, PFP84–AEHo11.

201. Eck and Childers, *Blueberry Culture,* 183.

202. Interview, Eugene Hunn with Brad Thompson and Bob Reeves, June 22, 1984, PFP84–AEHo12.

203. Cohen with Lee.

204. Interview, Rita Moonsammy with Margaret Bakely, December 23, 1985.

205. Ibid.

206. Cohen with Lee.

207. Moonsammy with Bakely.

208. Hunn with Thompson and Reeves, PFP84–AEHo12.

209. United States Immigration Commission, *Immigrants in Industries,* Part 24, *Recent Immigrants in Agriculture.* U.S. Senate Document No. 633, 61st Congress, 2d Session (Washington, D.C.: U.S. Government Printing Office, 1911) I: 72–73, 97.

210. Ibid.

211. Dieter Cunz, "Egg Harbor City: New Germany in New Jersey," New Jersey Historical Society *Proceedings* 73 (1955): 89–123.

212. U.S. Immigration Commission, *Recent Immigrants in Agriculture,* I: 63–65.

213. Interview, Jens Lund with Leonard Maglioccio, PFP83–RJLoo6.

214. Janet L. Donohue-McAdorey, "An Economic Analysis of Peach Production by Southern New Jersey Growers" (M.S. thesis, Rutgers University, 1984), 53–84.

215. Interview, Mal O'Connor with Ed Lamonaca, June 20, 1985, PFP85–AMOoo1.

216. Ibid.

217. Ibid.

218. J. Geraint Jenkins, *The English Farm Wagon: Origins and Structure* (Reading, England: Published by the Oakwood Press for the University of Reading, 1961).

219. Thomas F. Gordon, *A Gazetteer of the State of New Jersey* (Trenton: D. Fenton, 1834), 111.

220. Quoted in Bolger, Githens, and Rutsch, "Historic Architectural Survey," 17.

221. Isaac Mickle, *Reminiscences of Old Gloucester* (Philadelphia: Townsent Ward, 1845), 85.

222. *The Farm Journal and Farm Directory of Burlington County, N.J. 1913* (Philadelphia: Wilmer A. Kinson Co., 1913), 176.

223. Ibid.

224. Cunz, "Egg Harbor City."

225. U.S. Immigration Commission, *Immigrants in Agriculture,* I:51–60, 70–72, 90–92, 125, 129.

226. Ibid., II:89–144; Joseph Brandes, *Immigrants to Freedom; Jewish Communities in Rural New Jersey Since 1882* (Philadelphia: University of Pennsylvania Press, 1971); Edward S. Shapiro, "The Jews of New Jersey," in *The New Jersey Ethnic Experience,* ed. Barbara Cunningham (Union City: William S. Wise and Co., 1977), 294–311.

227. Interview, Rita Moonsammy with Bluma Purmell, July 1, 1985.

228. Shapiro, "The Jews of New Jersey," 303–304.

229. Pearl J. Lieff, "Types of Family Structure of Migrant Agricultural Workers" (Ph.D. dissertation, Rutgers University, 1971); Isham B. Jones, "The Puerto Rican Farm Worker in New Jersey," in *The Puerto Rican in New Jersey* (Trenton, NJ: New Jersey Department of Education, Division Against Discrimination, 1955), 14–20; Governor's Migrant Labor Task Force, *Seasonal Farm Workers in the State of New Jersey* (Seattle, WA: Consulting Services Corporation, 1968).

230. Interview, Christine Cartwright with Rae Gerber, November 1983, PFP83–RCC030.

231. Ibid.

232. Susan Samuelson, "The Landscape Experienced, Summary Statement for Phase II" (Pinelands Folklife Project, 1983), 5.

233. Interview, Christine Cartwright with Ephraim and Alice Tomlinson, October 18, 1983, PFP83–RCC016.

234. Interview, Rita Moonsammy with Rae Gerber, March 6, 1985.

235. Ibid.

236. Interview, Christine Cartwright with Rae Gerber, November 1983, PFP83–RCC029.

237. Pinelands Commission, *Comprehensive Management Plan for the Pinelands National Reserve . . .* (New Lisbon, NJ: Pinelands Commission, 1980), xvii.

INDEX